Heather Bahen
Box 6055, 9 Janet Drive
Janetville, Ontario
L0B 1K0

COWLEY PUBLICATIONS is a ministry of the brothers of the Society of Saint John the Evangelist, a monastic order in the Episcopal Church. Our mission is to provide books and resources for those seeking spiritual and theological formation. COWLEY PUBLICATIONS is committed to developing a new generation of writers and teachers who will encourage people to think and pray in new ways about spirituality, reconciliation, and the future.

~

D1510986

Trustworthy Connections

Trustworthy Connections
Interpersonal Issues in Spiritual Direction

∼

Anne Winchell Silver

COWLEY PUBLICATIONS
Cambridge, Massachusetts

Published in the United States of America by Cowley Publications,
a division of the Society of Saint John the Evangelist. No portion of
this book may be reproduced, stored in or introduced into a retrieval
system, or transmitted, in any form or by any means-including
photocopying-without the prior written permission of Cowley
Publications, except in the case of brief quotations embedded in
critical articles and reviews.

Library of Congress Cataloging-in-Publication Data:
Silver, Anne Winchell, 1948-
  Trustworthy connections : interpersonal issues in spiritual direction
/ Anne Winchell Silver.
    p. cm.
Includes bibliographical references.
  ISBN 1-56101-252-1 (pbk. : alk. paper)
  1. Spiritual direction. 2. Interpersonal relations—Religious
aspects—Christianity. I. Title.
  BV5053.S55 2004
  253.5'3—dc22
                                        2003027092

Scripture quotations are taken from The New Revised Standard
Version of the Bible, © 1989, by the Division of Christian Education
of the National Council of the Churches of Christ in the United States
of America. Used by permission.

Cover design: Gary Ragaglia

This book was printed in the United States of America on acid-free
paper.

COWLEY PUBLICATIONS
907 Massachusetts Avenue
Cambridge, Massachusetts 02139
800-225-1534 • www.cowley.org

For David

Your life was a blessing

Contents

Acknowledgements

This book came into being under difficult circumstances. While I was preparing it for publication, my husband, David, was diagnosed with cancer, received treatment, and died. I am profoundly grateful to everyone who sustained us with their prayers and caring during that indescribable time. Those who contributed most directly to the book include:

- William Doubleday, who inspired me to get this project started and helped it take shape;
- K. Jeanne Person and Jonathan Linman, whose thoughtful suggestions led to major revisions;
- Susan M. S. Brown, who guided the manuscript into its completed form;
- Jane Sullivan, Marilyn Anderson, Judith Brilliant, Ilene Rubenstein, Mary Ann Archer, Gayle Greene Watkins, Jane Gaeta, and Gillian Thomas, the spiritual direction and counseling colleagues who commented on early versions of these chapters;
- my peer supervision group, from whose shared experiences I derived many of the examples in the book;
- my directees, with whom and from whom I continue to learn most of what I know about spiritual direction;
- Audrey Williams, Pamela Bakal, Margaret Guenther, Douglas Brown, OHC, and Geoffrey Tristram, SSJE, who have served as models of spiritual direction for me;
- Rita W. Clark, from whom I learned about the healing power of good boundaries;

- Josh Silver, who provided the time and technology I needed to work on this book in the darkest of seasons;
- Marjorie and William Winchell, who were the first to show me what faith, commitment, and connection mean;

and especially
- David Bublick Silver, who supported me and cherished me and tried so hard to live long enough to see this book published.

Introduction

I never planned to be a spiritual director. In fact, I'd worked as a counselor in a large urban community college for a quarter of a century before I even realized that spiritual direction existed. For all those years I helped students consider the goals they wanted to pursue and figure out how to handle the psychological, educational, and socioeconomic challenges that might stand in the way of their achieving them. I even taught first-year seminars and courses called "career and life planning," in which I explained how to make career choices by assessing one's interests, abilities, and values; collecting information about jobs and the job market; examining personal circumstances; and then making carefully reasoned decisions based on all that information. I loved working with the students, had attained tenure and full professorship, and thought I'd try to stay at the college for another quarter of a century.

Hah. There was nothing carefully reasoned about what happened next. Somewhere around my twenty-eighth year on the job, I found myself unable to resist enrolling in a spiritual direction program at the General Theological Seminary's Center for Christian Spirituality. All of a sudden I was a fifty-year-old student with a subway pass and a backpack full of textbooks. Some of my friends and colleagues saw this move as a bold and admirable midlife transformation. Others thought I must be crazy. And none of them had ever heard of spiritual direction either, until I told them about it.

When I first felt called to offer spiritual direction, I was curious about how it differed from counseling and psychotherapy. My previous training had given me familiarity with treatment goals, diagnostic criteria, and solution-focused interventions. But from my experience of being a directee, it was clear to me that spiritual direction did not proceed along those lines at all. I was fascinated by the books that helped me learn about the prayerful, contemplative, and theological aspects of spiritual direction. I was awed by the idea that in the direction meeting, *God* is the real director. But even given divine involvement in the process, I supposed it wouldn't hurt for me to try to find out more about the down-to-earth framework of human relating within which spiritual direction takes place.

So I started searching through books for help with questions such as, "Do people get *paid* for doing this?" and, "When directees ask me questions about myself, how much is it appropriate to tell them?" and, "If a directee were to invite me to lunch, am I supposed to turn down the invitation?" I explored issues and problems that arise for directors and directees with respect to meeting space, payment, professionalization, boundaries, confidentiality, dual relationships, attraction, referral, the urge to "fix things," and the need for self-care. Because some of these topics were discussed so sparsely in the spiritual direction literature, I ended up drawing upon sources in the areas of pastoral care, counseling, psychotherapy, psychoanalysis, ethics, recovery programs, and congregational studies as well. I consulted experienced directors, visited Websites, listened to tapes of conference proceedings, and asked directees about their perceptions of the process. What eventually emerged was a compendium of "practical stuff I wish I'd known more about when I started to offer spiritual direction." When I began to talk about my findings, my colleagues seemed to think they were valuable, too. So I decided to write about them.

Some traditional and contemporary understandings about spiritual direction which underlie the discussions in this book are these:

* Unlike counseling or psychotherapy, the process of spiritual direction is focused not on technique and intervention by the director but rather on listening and discernment by both director and directee. Whereas a therapist might proceed according to a treatment plan, a spiritual director is likely to proceed deliberately without a plan, relying on God as the "real director."

- Spiritual direction is not a career choice or a job option. People who offer spiritual direction feel called by God to do so, and many do not accept payment for it.
- Spiritual directors may be clergy, members of religious orders, or laypeople from any walk of life. The ability to function as a spiritual director is not dependent on ordination or religious vows. I think that participation in some sort of training, formation, or enrichment program in spiritual direction is important, however.
- Spiritual direction is about growth in relationship to God, rather than about solving problems or fixing things. Some problems in a person's life may indeed be solved in the process, but that is not the goal or the focus.[1]

Although God is at the center of the process of spiritual direction, the more readily visible participants are human beings. Like all other people, directors and directees are subject to relationship dynamics. And the nature of that human interaction is likely to be at least as important as its verbal content. As one leader in the field of spiritual direction put it, "In the final analysis I believe that the most important thing in direction has relatively little to do with what is said, but a great deal to do with the quality of the relationship between director and directee."[2]

The topics and examples in this book are focused on traditional one-to-one, face-to-face spiritual direction, although some are relevant as well to other modalities, such as group direction and direction by correspondence. Chapters 1 through 9 begin with case examples, but the ensuing discussions are concerned less with the specifics of those examples than with the general issues they illustrate. Each chapter is designed to present a concise overview of points of view on the issue, rather than an exhaustive or in-depth analysis. Chapter 9 is addressed specifically to directees, discussing some basics about what to expect in spiritual direction and what to do if there seems to be a problem in the direction relationship. In chapter 10, I discuss ethical decision making and share some overall guidelines which emerged from my research and which I have found helpful in my work with directees. Two codes of ethics have been developed for spiritual directors, and those are included as appendixes. Finally, the sources I consulted are listed in an annotated bibliography for use in seeking further information.

All of the case examples are "real" in the sense that they represent situations that my colleagues and I have either experienced or heard about. But *none* of the examples is based on a single situation or person, and in *every* instance personal details have been carefully disguised and amalgamated.

This book was designed for use as a reference and a springboard for discussion for spiritual directors and anyone else who is interested in spiritual direction. The chapters follow a deliberate sequence, but understanding one chapter does not depend on having read previous chapters, so they need not be read in order. Please note that this book is in no way intended as a do-it-yourself manual or a substitute for training or supervision in spiritual direction. Rather, it is an attempt to identify some issues and challenges that can arise in spiritual direction relationships and to offer some resources for further consideration and reflection. Like the process of spiritual direction itself, this book is about asking questions, discussing ideas, and suggesting alternatives rather than giving advice or getting answers. And, like my ministry of spiritual direction, it is definitely a work in progress, open to debate and modification, and with growing edges all around.

Notes

1. For a much more complete discussion of what spiritual direction is and is not, see any of the following: Peter Ball, *Anglican Spiritual Direction* (Cambridge, MA: Cowley Publications, 1998); Tilden Edwards, *Spiritual Director, Spiritual Companion: Guide to Tending the Soul* (New York: Paulist Press, 2001); Margaret Guenther, *Holy Listening: The Art of Spiritual Direction* (Cambridge, MA: Cowley Publications, 1992); Gordon Jeff, *Spiritual Direction for Every Christian* (London: SPCK, 1987); Alan Jones, *Exploring Spiritual Direction: An Essay on Christian Friendship* (N.p.: Seabury Press, 1982); Kenneth Leech, *Soul Friend: A Study of Spirituality* (London: Sheldon Press, 1977); or Gerald G. May, *Care of Mind, Care of Spirit: A Psychiatrist Explores Spiritual Direction* (HarperSanFrancisco, 1992).

2. Jeff, *Spiritual Direction for Every Christian*, 73.

~

CHAPTER ONE

Sacred Space

ADAM AND BETH: *Adam is the rector of a small church in a rural area. He has no paid staff and runs the parish with the help of family members and volunteers. One way he tries to focus on prayer and contemplation amid all the practical demands of his position is to offer spiritual direction to Beth, a woman from a neighboring county.*

When Beth arrives for today's meeting, he greets her enthusiastically and removes a stack of hymnals from one of the chairs in his small, fluorescent-lit office to make room for her to sit. During the silence of their opening meditation, the telephone rings. Although a volunteer had been assigned to answer calls, the ringing continues until Adam finally mutters an apology and picks up the phone. As the meeting goes on, several parishioners peek in and wave at him through the window in his office door. Toward the end of the hour, a woman delivering a large cake for the congregation's centennial celebration walks into the office with it and reminds him that he'd promised to pay her on delivery.

CHARLOTTE AND ERICA: *Charlotte is a retired college professor who is beginning to offer spiritual direction. She had hoped to use a room in her church for this purpose, but the senior pastor is too worried about legal liability risks to be comfortable with such an arrangement. So she has converted her son's old bedroom into an office in her high-rise apartment. The renovated room looks inviting and comfortable, and she thinks that her pets, including Dietrich, her beloved Doberman pinscher, will lend yet another touch of warmth to the space. But when her first directee, Erica, arrives, it quickly becomes apparent that she is terrified of the dog. Their meeting is conducted with Charlotte and Erica locked in the office while Dietrich barks insistently just outside the door.*

FUMIKO AND GREGORY: *Fumiko, a layperson in a spiritual direction training program, is about to start offering spiritual direction. Her minister is supportive of her participation in the program and wants to provide her with a place in the church to meet with directees, but space is at a premium in the building. The only private room available is one in the basement that was formerly used to accommodate overflow Sunday school groups. During Fumiko's first meeting with her directee, Gregory, they peer at each other in the dim light and struggle to keep from toppling over in chairs built for kindergartners. From time to time their conversation is drowned out by clanking noises from the furnace in the corner.*

Offering a comfortable, quiet, secure place in which to meet is the first step in establishing a trustworthy connection. In her book on spiritual direction, Margaret Guenther characterized the physical arrangements for direction as a manifestation of hospitality: "What happens when we offer hospitality? We invite someone into a space that offers safety and shelter and put our own needs aside, as everything is focused on the comfort and refreshment of the guest. . . . Physical space is, in its way, as important as spiritual space."[1]

We are not disembodied souls that exist with no connection to the space we inhabit. Everything we do takes place in a physical context, and that context will have some effect on the quality of our experience. Therefore, if directees are to feel they can trust us to hear the deep secrets and longings of their souls, it is essential that we provide them with a suitable place in which to tell them.

THE POWER OF PLACE

At the most obvious level, the spiritual direction space should be as free as possible from conditions which might make the participants feel uncomfortable, unimportant, or unprotected. Directors and directees who are meeting in the presence of ringing phones, angry dogs, clanking furnaces, inappropriate furniture, poor lighting, or the possibility of someone else walking into the room are probably not going to be listening to each other, let alone to God, very effectively. Not only are such conditions distracting but they may also have unintended consequences for the direction relationship. A directee in Beth's situation might end up feeling resentful about all the interruptions or wonder whether she was taking time that Adam apparently needed to devote to more pressing concerns. Erica might have second thoughts about venturing into her spiritual director's apartment for subsequent meetings if she thinks the dog will be there, and Gregory might wonder why Fumiko's ministry in the church is so unimportant that it has been relegated to a corner of the basement.

More subtle aspects of context can influence the interaction as well. The effects of light, color, temperature, sounds, smells, familiarity, controllability, proximity to other people, and even electromagnetic fields are now being examined by means of an emerging interdisciplinary approach called "the science of place." Research in this area is concerned with the ways people's emotions and behaviors are influenced by elements in the physical world around them, often on a level outside their awareness. Observations that have emerged from these studies include the following:

- We learn to associate our experiences with the physical conditions under which they occur. For example, habits and addictions are much more dependent on environmental cues than was once thought.

- We are most likely to remember something we learned in the place where we first learned it. (Whenever I go to get something and forget what it was by the time I get there, I return to the place where I originally thought of it, and some cue in the environment usually serves as a reminder.)
- "Warm" colors (e.g., red) tend to be stimulating, and "cool" colors (e.g., blue) may have a calming effect.
- Variations in quantity of illumination produce variations in the level of the hormone melatonin, resulting in arousal or sleepiness. An extreme example of this phenomenon is seasonal affective disorder, in which the relative lack of light in winter triggers severe depression in some people.
- Temperature also affects level of arousal. Cold tends to be stimulating, and heat tends to be sedating. (During my years as a community college teacher, I would turn on lights and fling open windows when a class seemed to be losing focus.)
- Noise is the most disruptive environmental distractor. (I am reminded of the time a jackhammer operator began digging up the sidewalk outside the church during a parish quiet day.)
- The more uncontrollable and unpredictable the distractor or stressor, the more negative its effects.
- Attempting to shut out distractions drains energy.[2]

What do factors such as these have to do with spirituality? The nineteenth-century communities of the Shakers exemplified ways in which physical elements can be used to express spiritual values. In their efforts to convey their collective "enlightened spirit" and create a taste of "heaven on earth" that would attract converts, the Shakers turned away from the era's prevailing affection for dark, closed-in, cluttered interiors and instead created spaces for people and livestock that were replete with natural light, air, simplicity, and symmetry.[3] As one artist commented, "There were no dark corners in those lives. Their religion thrived on light . . ."[4]

It appears that environmental factors even affect how we see and judge things. In *The Experience of Place*, Tony Hiss described an experiment by the psychologist Abraham Maslow and associates that compared perceptions and judgments made in rooms set up to be variously "beautiful," "average," and "ugly." The study participants in the attractive, well-appointed experiment room were noticeably more likely to describe a series of photographs of human faces as showing "energy" and "well-being" than were those who viewed the same photographs in the ugly room or the average room. Even the behavior of the interviewers who performed the study was found to be affected by the room they used—and neither the participants nor the interviewers were aware that apparently it was the décor that was affecting their judgment or their work.[5]

How does a room look to a person who walks into it? According to the ancient Chinese principles of *feng shui*, what people see when they enter a place will influence what happens there.[6] What type of setting would we like our directees to find when they come to meet with us? According to the Center for Sacred Psychology's *Code of Ethics for Spiritual Directors* (see appendix 1), "Spiritual direction sessions should take place in an environment of privacy, peacefulness and safety. . . . The ideal is that the period of spiritual direction be a protected time, a 'Sabbath-time,' in a nourishing, oasis-like space that speaks to the directee of first priorities. . . . When coming for spiritual direction, directees should be able to trust that their time is dedicated to them."

Here, then, are some of the most important environmental factors for spiritual direction:

* Accessibility.
  People who use mobility aids or have difficulty climbing stairs should be made as welcome in our spiritual direction space as those who do not.

* Privacy, safety, and freedom from interruptions.
Spiritual direction is a time of prayer. Directees should feel
that we will be paying close attention to them and to God
during the meeting.
* Quiet, or at least a relative lack of auditory distractions.
* Moderate temperature and lighting.
Although moderation usually seems preferable with respect
to these environmental elements, there are times when
strong or subdued lighting can be beneficial (to offset a de-
pressed mood or to calm anxiety, respectively). For example, I have had exceptionally fruitful meetings in a
Sunday school room where the sunlight that streamed
through the wall-to-wall windows on a winter morning
seemed to make the warmth of God's love an undeniable
physical reality.
* Choice of appropriate seating.
When a friend of mine walked into her director's office for
the first time, the director stood at the door while my
friend tried anxiously to figure out where she was "supposed" to sit. With her experience in mind, when a directee
comes into the room I make sure to say that she or he is
welcome to sit anywhere. Whenever possible, I like to have
three chairs in the room, as a reminder of the presence of
the divine as well as a way of providing a range of seating
choices.
* Lack of clutter.
For most of us the world is already cluttered enough, and
spiritual direction can offer some needed respite and refreshment. Rooms that are minefields of defunct office equip-
ment, dusty knickknacks, and teetering stacks of papers may
make it more difficult to focus and clear our minds.
* A carefully chosen sensory aid or two.
A lighted candle, a picture, a religious object, incense, or
something that represents the natural world (my spiritual
director suggests water, salt, and wheat) can help us iden-

tify the spiritual direction meeting as a time set apart for contemplation and serve as a reminder of the presence of God. (It is advisable to check with directees before lighting candles or incense, however, in case of allergies or discomfort with fire.) Inviting directees to bring an object to focus on can be especially effective. One of the most moving direction meetings I have ever had took place in the presence of a small, battered wooden donkey that a directee brought in to represent her spiritual self.

Perhaps Tilden Edwards's suggestions about physical environment as an ingredient of the spiritual direction conversation provide the best summary: "The simpler, quieter, and more aesthetically warm the room," he wrote, "the more your space might invite a simpler, quieter, more easeful presence."[7]

REALITY FACTORS

Unfortunately, spiritual directors may not always have an optimal amount of control over the environments in which they meet with directees. Clergy, parish staff members, and members of religious orders, whose pastoral responsibilities generally afford them access to appropriate rooms in their parishes, convents, or monasteries, may have few difficulties. For laypeople who are not officially employed in churches, however, finding an "oasis-like space" can be more of a challenge. Competing demands for space in churches are one problem that laypeople may encounter; concerns about the church's liability if the director were to be sued for misconduct are another.

Sometimes it seems there is just no room at the inn. My lay colleagues and I have conducted spiritual direction meetings in a wide array of borrowed church offices. On the occasions when those were not available to us, we have resorted to Sunday school rooms, sacristies, choir lofts, naves, rehearsal rooms, parish hall parlors, kitchens, basements, storage rooms, churchyards, gardens, parks, seashores, sidewalk benches, restaurants, and automobiles. Our meetings in those venues have been interrupted by sextons, Sunday school teachers, acolytes, altar guild members, florists, electricians, homeless people, bicyclists, waiters, children, dogs, insects, thunderstorms, a prospective bridal couple, a chef, and a man washing his car. These peripatetic adventures did serve to remind us that "the earth is the Lord's, and everything in it," and more than occasionally some aspect of such an environment has turned out to be a source of inspiration. However, the quiet, privacy, and safety of a conventional office setting is more reliably conducive to spiritual reflection.

If no appropriate church space is available, where can we go? Home offices are the most obvious alternatives, but complicating factors are by no means limited to unruly pets. Offices at home raise safety questions for both directee and director. For example, what reservations might a young female directee feel about going alone to the home of a male director she has not yet met? What concerns might a director have about being alone at home with a relative stranger, or about the possibility of being sued by a litigious individual? Working at home also poses potential distractions for the director. As Margaret Guenther put it, "I find that I cannot see people for spiritual direction in my home: there is too much confusion of roles and personae. . . . the impedimenta of daily living intrude and make the space so personal that our appointment threatens to turn into a friendly chat."[8]

Other options for laypeople include arranging to use space in other churches or religious organizations; meeting in one's workplace; borrowing space in a friend's professional office; or renting an office. This last option in particular, however, entails significant expense and therefore raises another issue, that of payment for spiritual direction (see chapter 3).

Notes

1. Margaret Guenther, *Holy Listening: The Art of Spiritual Direction* (Cambridge, MA: Cowley Publications, 1992), 14.

2. List derived from Winifred Gallagher, *The Power of Place: How Our Surroundings Shape Our Thoughts, Emotions, and Actions* (New York: Poseidon Press, 1993); and Tony Hiss, *The Experience of Place* (New York: Vintage Books, 1991), 34.

3. Gallagher, *Power of Place*, 47–48.

4. Ibid., 48, quoting the painter Charles Sheeler.

5. Hiss, *Experience of Place*, 38–40.

6. Gallagher, *Power of Place*, 143, quoting the *feng shui* practitioner Sarah Rossbach.

7. Tilden Edwards, *Spiritual Director, Spiritual Companion: Guide to Tending the Soul* (New York: Paulist Press, 2001), 109.

8. Guenther, *Holy Listening*, 14–15.

◠

CHAPTER TWO

Covenant

HAL AND MONSIGNOR IGNATIUS: *Driving to his second spiritual direction meeting, Hal is decidedly anxious. At their first meeting his director, Monsignor Ignatius, had seemed imposing and stern, and Hal had felt so self-conscious that he'd tripped on the fringes of the Oriental rug and knocked over a small statue as they walked into the office. As soon as they were seated, the priest had bowed his head, closed his eyes, and remained silent for what seemed like a long time while his directee glanced surreptitiously around the room and tried to guess what was going to happen next. After the silence ended, Hal had attempted to describe the spiritual issues that concerned him, but his account suddenly seemed incoherent to him. When Hal had asked whether or how much payment was expected for spiritual direction, Ignatius had shrugged his shoulders and said, "Make an offering." Hal knows that this spiritual director is a friend of the priest who referred him, and he wonders whether Ignatius has yet told his priest what a spiritual dunce he is. The more he thinks about the previous meeting, the more he wonders whether he should just turn around and go home.*

JOANNE AND KIRSTEN: *Joanne has been going to Kirsten for spiritual direction for several months. At one point during their last meeting, Kirsten made reference to "you and your children." Joanne does not have any children and thought her director must have confused some details of her life with those of another directee. But she didn't want to embarrass Kirsten by mentioning the error, so she let it pass. Days later, however, Joanne finds she is still thinking about it and is concerned about how well Kirsten really understands her. She wonders how Kirsten will react if she brings up this issue in their next meeting.*

～

It is easy for us to assume that people who are interested enough in spiritual direction to seek out a director already know what to expect from the process. And it is tempting to assume that the less structure and the fewer rules we set up to govern our direction relationships, the more unencumbered our interactions will be and the more freely God's spirit will be able to move.

But can we still recall what it was like for us to be new directees? Even if our first spiritual directors seemed welcoming and unthreatening, can we remember feeling at all vulnerable or awkward? Were we unclear about what we were supposed to do or reluctant to say what was on our minds? People often approach direction feeling uncertain about why, exactly, they are there, or whether they ought to be there at all. They may have only vague or inaccurate ideas about what goes on in spiritual direction. They may imagine that they are coming to meet with a person who is considerably more "holy" than themselves. They may be worried about appearing ignorant or doing something wrong. They may, like Hal, be afraid that they will be found to be "spiritual dunces." They may wonder what their director might say about them to people they know. If directees are to relax and feel safe enough with us to explore their spiritual questions with any degree of honesty, they need to know what to expect and what the norms of the arrangement will be.

Certainly it is true that the process of spiritual direction is likely to be hindered by the inflexible application of a lot of complicated rules. But a defined structure need not be a legalistic straitjacket. In any helping relationship, explicitly understood "boundaries—of space, time, financial structure, and limits on personal sharing—help to secure the 'safe space' within which mutual respect can take place."[1] A recurring theme in this book will be that a modest number of well-chosen, carefully thought out, and mutually agreed upon guidelines facilitate, rather than restrict, growth within the spiritual direction process.

Spiritual Directors International recommends that its *Guidelines for Ethical Conduct* (see appendix 2) be used by directors and directees at the outset of their relationship to discuss and agree on the nature of spiritual direction, the roles and responsibilities of director and directee, the length and frequency of meetings, payment or other compensation, and evaluation and termination processes. The Center for Sacred Psychology's *Code of Ethics for Spiritual Directors* (see appendix 1) adds that directors should ask new directees whether they have previously been in spiritual direction, counseling, or psychotherapy, and should ask any directee currently in counseling or therapy to obtain that practitioner's approval for the spiritual direction arrangement.[2]

The first few direction meetings are a time of discernment and clarification. In addition to the essential task of determining whether director and directee are a good enough match to continue to work together, topics that might be discussed include these:

* What spiritual direction is and is not.
  What are the directee's needs, hopes, and expectations? Is spiritual direction the best way to address them at this time? Are there approaches or resources (e.g., therapy, support groups, Bible study programs, prayer groups, healing services) that might be utilized in addition to or instead of direction? Shalem Institute for Spiritual Forma-

tion's online pamphlet about spiritual direction (http://www.shalem.org/sd.html) includes a helpful section titled "If Not Direction, Then What?"

* God and prayer in spiritual direction.
  The focus of the direction process on prayer and relationship with God, rather than on personal problem solving, should be clarified. The belief that God is the "real director" might be given particular attention, as might the idea that praying is something which is actually done, as well as discussed, during spiritual direction meetings.

* Focus on directee.
  Although the director may share his or her own experiences from time to time, the directee's experiences and concerns are to be the focus of attention.

* Confidentiality and privacy.
  The directee should be assured that everything she or he tells the director will be kept in strict confidence, with a few specific exceptions (see further discussion of confidentiality in the next section).

* Meeting schedule.
  How frequent are the meetings to be, and how long will each meeting last? What are the procedures for cancelations, rescheduling, and lateness?

* Payment.
  Is the directee expected to offer some form of material compensation in exchange for the director's time or expertise? If so, how much, in what form, and how and when is it to be given? What if the directee has difficulty paying the fee? (See chapter 3 for further discussion of payment.)

* Contact between meetings.
  What, if any, contact between scheduled meetings will be considered appropriate? Will telephone calls or e-mail messages be acceptable? If so, will there be any limit on their frequency? (See chapter 4 for discussion of relationships outside the context of spiritual direction.)

* Other expectations.
  What other expectations need to be made clear at the outset? For example, some directors will work only with directees who make a commitment to participate regularly in some sort of worshiping community, or intend to make periodic sacramental confessions.
* Ending the relationship.
  What happens if either participant feels the time may have come to terminate the relationship?

CONFIDENTIALITY

The topic of confidentiality in spiritual direction is so important that it warrants further discussion. Writing about the ideal conditions for spiritual direction, Sister Linda Julian of the Order of St. Helena indicated that "good boundaries are essential for the development of real trust. The commitment to confidentiality on the part of the director must be the same as for anyone who hears confessions. As a directee, you must be free to talk about absolutely anything, or not much depth will be reached, or much way made for the action of the Holy Spirit."[3]

Spiritual direction is like confession because of the often deeply personal, intimate nature of what is discussed. The sharing of sensitive information has the potential to arouse feelings on both sides that must be handled with great care and respect, especially in the context of small communities. The pastoral theology professor William Doubleday once commented, "There is much sloppy talk in the Episcopal Church about what people said to or heard from their spiritual directors or confessors, and there are too many confessors, spiritual directors, and pastors who have an insufficiently high doctrine of confidentiality."[4]

Breaches of confidentiality probably arise more often from the impulse to gossip than from outright malice. It seems to be characteristic of human nature to want to discuss what we know with other people or to be bearers of "inside" information. Spiritual directors, like everyone else, are subject to being affected by what people tell us and to feeling tempted to pass it on. And even if we are utterly committed to preserving confidentiality, problems can still arise if we lose track of the context in which we heard something. According to Margaret Guenther, "The safest path for me has been the cultivation of amnesia, even about 'harmless' details, since it is difficult to remember where I first heard bits of news about jobs, pregnancies, crises, and triumphs."[5]

The directives for confidentiality extend beyond promising not to reveal the content of what directees tell us. According to *A Code of Ethics for Spiritual Directors*, "Spiritual directors do not reveal the names of those whom they serve in this capacity, past or present, nor do they allude to them in conversation (even anonymously as 'a sister' or 'someone who comes to me for direction')."

The code does set forth two exceptions to the rule of confidentiality: the discussion of case material in supervision, and the reporting of situations in which serious danger or harm is involved or threatened. With respect to the first exception, directees are to be informed that the director is receiving supervision and assured that their anonymity will be preserved. With respect to the second, directors are morally obligated to see that suicidal persons act upon referrals to mental health professionals and might also "contact family members of the person at risk, preferably with that person's cooperation"; and "Where there is clear danger to another's safety or life (e.g., child abuse), spiritual directors, like all citizens, have a duty to warn the endangered parties or their legal guardians, and are morally responsible to intervene by reporting such danger to the proper authorities."

Although confidentiality is imperative for us as directors, it should be noted that our directees are not bound by the same requirement. As *A Code of Ethics for Spiritual Directors* puts it, "Directees should be encouraged to maintain reticence about the content of sessions, out of respect for the sacredness of the interior life. . . . This is, however, a recommendation to the person seeking guidance and is not obligatory (as is the director's confidentiality)."

DEMYSTIFICATION

For some first-time directees, the very prospect of spiritual direction may seem intimidating. Gordon Jeff, founding member of a British network for the promotion of spiritual direction, commented that "our potential directee . . . knows that he or she will need to be talking about intensely personal matters, about weakness and failure and guilt, and in nine cases out of ten admitting to an inadequate prayer life or perhaps a prayer life which has broken down completely."[6] One of my own concerns as a new directee had been that my not entirely orthodox religious and spiritual history might seem peculiar (if not heretical) to a clergyperson in a mainstream denomination, and it took even my highly approachable and accepting director several meetings to convince me otherwise.

"And on top of this," Jeff continued, "an experienced director, unfamiliar except by reputation, may well be seen as an authoritative, even condemning figure."[7] Indeed, it is not entirely clear whether Monsignor Ignatius is as imposing a person as Hal seems to have found him, or whether the problem is more that Hal was overawed by his director's title, clerical garb, office decor, silent prayerfulness, or lack of explicitness about what to expect. Particularly if spiritual directors are clergy or members of religious orders, it is easy enough for directees, unconsciously or even consciously, to experience their directors as representatives of the divine, or as parental or other authority figures. It is, of course, important that directees respect us and view us as offering experience and guidance that is of value; otherwise, new directors working in their own parishes or communities can have experiences that are all too reminiscent of the reception Jesus received in his home town in Matthew 13:55–58. But a directee who regards the director as some sort of flawless or superior being may have trouble being candid enough to explore difficult issues very deeply.

Here are some ways in which my colleagues in spiritual direction have told me they try to demystify their roles and seem more approachable:

- Having directees address them by their given names
- Revealing things about themselves (e.g., difficulties, feelings, "growing edges") where appropriate
- Dressing somewhat informally
- Candidly admitting it when they don't know something
- Answering questions about their family or personal life where appropriate

Gordon Jeff pointed out that the difference between therapy and spiritual direction proves especially useful at the outset: the director is freer than a therapist to reveal information about himself or herself and so can more easily be seen as a real, human, imperfect person. "A little time of general chat [in the first meeting] will help both sides to lose some of the wrong projections, to begin by meeting simply as two human individuals and start building up a relationship."[8]

Demystification efforts such as these are useful only as long as they are consistent with the director's own personality and do not seem contrived. For instance, if Monsignor Ignatius is not comfortable with dressing less formally or talking about himself during spiritual direction meetings, he should not do so. Another caution about demystification is that any moves toward informality and openness should not shade over into the territory of inappropriate relationships (see chapter 4) or of talking too much about oneself (see chapter 8).

Perhaps demystification is an important *internal* process for spiritual directors as well. Whenever a meeting with a directee seems to have gone especially well and I start to feel as if I might be developing into some sort of wonderful spiritual guru, I remind myself of one of the definitions of spiritual direction, attributed to Benedict J. Groeschel, that I learned in my training program: "Spiritual direction is two poor sinners sitting down together."

A SAMPLE COVENANT

The covenant I have developed to use in individual spiritual direction follows the basic guidelines just discussed and includes a few additional elements I have derived from my own experiences of counseling and being counseled. This covenant is not a written document that I hand to the directee the minute she or he first walks in the door but rather an unwritten set of procedures and expectations that I make sure we talk about during our first meeting or two and revisit periodically. It is intended not as a hard and fast set of rules but rather a collection of guidelines that we both resolve to follow. Problems with or exceptions to any of its elements are open to discussion at any point in the relationship.

A typical agreement with my directees includes these elements:

* Count on confidentiality.
  From the outset, I (the director) promise not to reveal or discuss any aspect of our conversations, with two exceptions: if there is a credible threat of serious harm, or to receive supervision. In the latter case, I will not do so without securing permission or carefully disguising identity and circumstances.
* No strings attached.
  I expect no direct payment or gifts in exchange for spiritual direction. A directee may make a donation to my parish or other charitable organization if he or she feels moved to do so, but the donation will have no influence on our relationship. (See chapter 3 for discussion of other positions on the question of payment.)
* No socializing.
  Both of us will strive to keep our spiritual direction rela-

tionship singular and unique by limiting contact outside the direction meetings. (See chapter 4 for discussion of other positions on this question.)

* Respect each other's time.
We both agree to do our best to begin and end meetings on time and to notify each other of requested changes to our appointment schedule as soon as possible.

* Begin and end meetings with prayer.
We mark the beginning and ending of each meeting with a few minutes of silence and/or spoken prayer and/or words from Scripture. Either of us, or both, may offer spoken prayer or readings during these intervals.

* Call prayer breaks as needed.
A spiritual direction meeting is a time of prayer throughout. Either of us may request a pause in the conversation for silent reflection or spoken prayer whenever moved to do so.

* Tell the truth.
Within the space of our direction meetings, several of the ordinary conventions of conversation are suspended. I assure the directee that if I say anything that is hurtful or upsetting or seems off-base, I want to hear about that reaction. If I say something that is inaccurate, as Kirsten did, the directee should have no qualms about pointing that out. Likewise, if I think she or he may be on the wrong track about something, I will say so. We will do our best to offer each other constructive feedback without worrying about having to be "nice" or saying only what we think the other person wants to hear.

* Ask anything.
This is another suspension of the rules of polite conversation. The directee should not think there is any question that is too "stupid," personal, or inappropriate to ask. It is my responsibility to figure out how to deal with any question, and to do so nonjudgmentally.

- Honor non sequiturs.
  This the third departure from ordinary conversational norms. If a thought occurs to either of us that does not seem to fit logically into the discussion, we should express it anyway. It could be the inspiration of God at work.
- Pray for each other.
  We resolve to keep each other in our prayers between meetings. In addition, I make a commitment to spend time in prayer about the directee in preparation for, and after, each of our meetings.
- Consider how we're doing.
  Every so often (once or twice a year), we set aside some time to look for evidence of the fruits of the relationship for the directee and decide whether it is time to try different approaches, continue as is, or terminate the relationship.

Notes

1. Karen Lebacqz and Ronald G. Barton, "Boundaries, Mutuality, and Professional Ethics," in *Boundary Wars: Intimacy and Distance in Healing Relationships*, ed. Katherine Hancock Ragsdale (Cleveland: Pilgrim Press, 1996), 103.

2. For a contrasting view of the recommendation to seek the mental health practitioner's approval, see Gerald G. May, "Professionalizing Spiritual Direction," *Shalem News On Line* 24:3 (Fall 2000), http://www.shalem.org/sn/24.3gm.html.

3. Linda Julian, "On Finding a Spiritual Director," *Quarterly Newsletter of the Order of St. Helena* 20:1 (March 1999), 1; available at http://www.osh.org/ministries/Ministries(LJarticle).

4. William A. Doubleday, "Response to Bishop Taylor," *The Anglican* (October 1998), 20.

5. Margaret Guenther, *Holy Listening: The Art of Spiritual Direction* (Cambridge, MA: Cowley Publications, 1992), 19.

6. Gordon Jeff, *Spiritual Direction for Every Christian* (London: SPCK, 1987), 27.

7. Ibid.

8. Ibid.

~

CHAPTER THREE

Payment

LENNY: *Lenny is a high school social studies teacher who has been exploring options for a career change for some time. As part of that process, he is in a spiritual direction training program. His wife and several of their friends are psychologists in private practice, so he asks them for advice on setting up arrangements to met with directees. All of them tell him that he should charge a fee for his services, even if on a sliding scale, because clients are much more likely to value and work hard in a helping relationship if they pay for it. Lenny knows that most people in his program believe that spiritual direction is a gift, not a business, but he cannot help thinking that charging fees would help him establish his professional status in the field. Besides, his wife and friends assure him, no-fee arrangements would make his directees feel guilty and obligated.*

MARIA: *Maria is an occupational therapist who has been offering spiritual direction one or two evenings a week in her church for several years. Recently she cut back her hours at the nursing home where she works in order to have time to see more directees. She is usually able to make ends meet on the reduced income, even though her activities as a spiritual director involve significant overhead, including insurance cov-*

erage, parking fees, travel to peer supervision group meetings, spiritual direction organization dues, and workshops and courses she takes to supplement what she learned in her training program. She does not charge for spiritual direction because she believes it is a gift or charism. But whenever unexpected bills crop up, she has to work more hours in the nursing home when she would prefer to be doing more direction. She is beginning to wonder whether it would be appropriate to ask her directees to pay her just enough to cover her expenses.

NORMAN AND OLGA: *Norman is a freelance editor and writer who works at home. He also has been offering spiritual direction in his home for several years. His directees pay him on a sliding scale of $25 to $60 per hour. Olga, a directee with whom he has been meeting for the past three months, left her secretarial job in search of some other form of livelihood and is now finding it difficult to support herself, let alone pay for spiritual direction. She asks whether they might work out a barter arrangement until she has a steady income again. For each hour Norman spends with her for spiritual direction, Olga proposes to spend an hour organizing his home office.*

～

Payment and professionalization are probably the most hotly debated issues in the field of spiritual direction today. The tradition of spiritual direction in Western Christianity began with people seeking counsel from monastics who had extensive experience in the spiritual life. Until relatively recently it continued as a function of members of religious orders and clergy, mostly Roman Catholic. Only in the last thirty years or so have Protestants and laypeople begun offering direction in significant numbers. As the population of clergy and religious declines and the interest in spiritual direction increases, laypeople have become more widely accepted in this role. This is probably one of the reasons that questions of payment and professionalization have arisen.[1]

Payment, like meeting space, is an issue that tends to affect lay directors disproportionately. Clergy and members of religious orders who offer spiritual direction generally do so as part of their pastoral responsibilities and so are less likely to be concerned with receiving direct compensation; directees who wish to express their appreciation monetarily usually make offerings to the director's church, convent, or monastery. In contrast, most laypeople who serve as spiritual directors do so in addition to holding down paying jobs in other fields or relying on other sources of livelihood. Spiritual direction traditionally has not been regarded as a means of supporting oneself, but lately there are many who are attempting to do just that.

The recent trend toward professionalization of spiritual direction is evident from the existence of many formal training or formation programs, a professional association (Spiritual Directors International), and at least two codes of ethics. As Robert Willis noted, "Gone are the images of spiritual directors as sequestered holy people living in earthen cells, . . . monkshoods pulled securely over heads to drive away the permeating chill."[2] Nowadays, a spiritual director might be found attending a workshop on how to build a spiritual direction practice or reading an article on how to drum up business with ads, brochures, speaking engagements, and gift certificates.[3] Writing about spiritual direction in the Anglican tradition, Peter Ball noted that "divisions over questions of training, qualification, and accreditation among leading people in the world of spiritual direction run deep. Pressure about payments, insurance, security, professional standards, and oversight confronts a deeply held belief in spiritual direction as a response to a God-given vocation, where the gifts and skills required are seen primarily as charism."[4]

The question of whether it is appropriate to request payment for spiritual direction is a complicated one. The most frequently offered arguments and counterarguments about payment are outlined in the "Payment for Spiritual Direction?" table, found on the next page.

PAYMENT FOR SPIRITUAL DIRECTION?
PROS AND CONS

PRO	CON
Isn't it always better to have more money?	How much is "enough"?
People in this society are respected in proportion to how much money they can command.	Is spiritual direction about commanding personal respect?
Charging fees helps establish a professional relationship	Is spiritual direction about establishing ourselves as professionals?
People won't value or apply themselves seriously to spiritual direction if they don't pay.	There seem to be many exceptions to this supposed rule (see note).
Getting something for nothing may make a directee feel uneasy, obligated, guilty, resentful, dependent, or "one-down."	Getting something for nothing may also have healing potential. Besides, there are other ways to deal with those responses.
People who offer a service without being compensated may arouse suspicion because they are behaving counterculturally.	Then Jesus was an excellent role model.
People who offer a service without being compensated may become resentful.	Resentment is less likely for people who are clear about their reasons for not accepting compensation.
Reluctance to charge fees may signal a lack of self-confidence or a reaction against unconscious greed.	Or it might not.
If directees are unable to pay a fee, bartering arrangements are an alternative.	Bartering arrangements may lead to problems in the relationship.
Many spiritual directors have invested considerable time, money, and effort to equip themselves for this ministry.	

PRO	CON
Many spiritual directors incur ongoing expenses in this ministry (e.g., supervision, insurance, continuing education).	
The income tax deductions for expenses for paid work are more favorable than for volunteer work.	
Directors who don't have to hold outside jobs to support themselves have more time for directees.	
Charging a fee may help keep the interaction from shading over into a social relationship.	
	Payment changes the dynamics of the relationship.
	Payment may foster a "fix-it" or "get-results" mentality in the director and/or the directee.
	Payment affects legal liability and may increase the likelihood of lawsuits.
	Individual directees usually meet with us for only one hour per month. How much of that time do we want to dedicate to negotiating, collecting, and renegotiating fees?

Note: The belief, originally articulated by Sigmund Freud, that people don't take helping relationships seriously if they don't pay for them has become less generally accepted in recent years. See, for example, Alan B. Tulipan, "Fee Policy as an Extension of the Therapist's Style and Orientation," in *The Last Taboo: Money as Symbol and Reality in Psychotherapy and Psychoanalysis*, ed. David W. Krueger (New York: Brunner/Mazel, 1986), 80, 81; and Rosalea A. Schonbar, "The Fee as Focus of Transference and Countertransference in Treatment," in *Last Taboo*, 38.

FEES, OFFERINGS, STIPENDS, REIMBURSEMENTS, OR BARTERING?

What are people actually paying for when they give money in exchange for spiritual direction? Is it the director's expertise and/or training? Or the director's time? Or is it reimbursement for the director's expenses? A variety of answers have been offered.

Directors who define themselves as professionals, as Lenny has been advised to do, generally consider their directees to be compensating them for their expertise and training. This definition places spiritual direction within the framework of our society's service economy. As one ethicist commented about professionalism in general, "Within the professional arena the buyer, or client, is remunerating the professional for her or his intellectual and technical skills. To be a professional within an advanced capitalist society is to provide a rationalized technical skill to buyers within the prevailing institutionalized economic framework."[5] In some communities or denominations, it is customary for spiritual directors to be paid, and there is some traditional support for doing so.

But not everyone is comfortable with such an arrangement in an endeavor in which God is considered to be the actual director. Here are some other ways people have framed or conceptualized the exchange of money for spiritual direction:

* Charging for "time" rather than for expertise.
  Addressing clergy, the social ethicist Karen Lebacqz and the spirituality professor Joseph D. Driskill suggested, "Where one's time is covered by the general job description in a church, it is already paid. Where one's time is not covered by the general job description in a church, it is not already paid and should be compensated."[6]
* Charging for expenses rather than for time or expertise, as Maria is thinking of doing.
  As Peter Ball expressed it, "People do give me money—not as a fee, but to help towards my expenses."[7]

- Receiving payment indirectly (as when a directee gives an offering to the parish and then the parish remits all or a portion of that payment to the director).
- Receiving stipends from a parish or other organization.

Beyond the question of whether to charge money is that of how much to charge. In an article on this topic in *Presence*, the journal of Spiritual Directors International, Bill Creed quoted a letter from a director who asked:

> Why is it that I am "worth" anywhere between $5 and $20 for an hour [as a spiritual director], when a therapist gets between $40 and $100, a masseuse $50, etc., etc.? When I taught piano I received $35 to $50 an hour. Why, when the Spirit calls me to this incredibly wonderful work of spiritual guidance, do I get penalized for it, in the world's terms?[8]

Creed then offered two hypothetical responses, one from a "spiritual direction minister" and one from a "spiritual direction professional." The "minister" tells the writer of the letter that "the 'world' does not value spiritual direction and spiritual directors do not value the 'world's' values" and reminds her that "in reality, the Spirit is the director."[9] The "professional" director, by contrast, assures the letter writer that "the courage to ask your directees for a just compensation is an exercise of your professional responsibility and one way to affirm your value" and that "when you set a just fee, you admit that God does not write checks to pay for room and board but rather empowers you to support yourself."[10]

But how do we determine what constitutes "a just compensation"? One interesting solution to this question was suggested to me by Elizabeth Holland, a spiritual director who said she asks each directee what he or she earns per hour, and that amount ordinarily becomes that person's fee. Other directors have set up sliding scales or fee ranges. Some who wish to avoid charging a set fee or stipend request a free-will offering. For example, a two-person spiritual direction ministry in Illinois reported that "at the initial interview we simply ask for an 'offering' for the ministry, suggest a range, and then leave it entirely up to the individual."[11]

Still others enter into bartering or exchange-of-services arrangements with directees for whom cash payment would constitute a hardship. Such arrangements ought to be approached cautiously and evaluated carefully in light of their potential to complicate or compromise the direction relationship, however. In *Keeping Boundaries: Maintaining Safety and Integrity in the Psychotherapeutic Process*, Richard S. Epstein noted that "therapists have been known to permit their patients to perform skilled services such as accounting, secretarial work, home construction, and legal services in return for treatment. This situation usually involves an increasing personal involvement between patient and therapist" and sometimes precedes more inappropriate forms of involvement.[12] For instance, what effect might Olga's working in Norman's home have on their relationship? How well can Norman, who has met with her only three times, evaluate how such an arrangement is likely to work out? Could Olga's suggestion of the bartering arrangement reflect a wish to move the relationship in a more personal direction?

LEGAL IMPLICATIONS

Without delving too far into the legal ramifications of the issue of payment, I will simply note that receiving payment or bartering services may alter the legal landscape of the direction relationship. As Karen Lebacqz and Joseph Driskill explained, "Charging fees implies that one is providing a 'professional' service and should have the requisite training, supervision, and structured practice. In this litigious society, people who are professionally trained and charge fees are subject to closer scrutiny from a legal vantage point."[13] Another author asked: "When the director sets a fee, what does the director legally bind oneself to do and not do?" and "When the director only seeks a donation or offers direction without monetary reward, is the director less bound legally?"[14]

Bartering or exchanging services has the potential to give rise to even more legal complications in relation to, for example, fairness of the exchange and adequate performance of services. For example, how might Norman's spiritual direction relationship with Olga be affected if her organization of his office falls short of his expectations? If Olga feels she is putting more effort into her side of the exchange than Norman is, how might that influence their interaction? And what of the implications for confidentiality if she comes across information about his other directees while sorting through his paperwork?

Not receiving compensation for spiritual direction may lessen the probability that directees will be inclined to sue us. However, it is important to remember that there is no way to guarantee that even the most competent, conscientious, ethical director will never have legal action taken against him or her by a disgruntled directee. Practically anyone can file a lawsuit about practically anything against practically anyone. The only way to be immune from litigation arising from offering spiritual direction is never to have offered spiritual direction! (And even then, I suppose, a person might be sued for direction *not* offered.) Spiritual direction, like any other relationship, will always entail some risk. The best way to minimize that risk is to hold ourselves to the highest standard of ethical conduct.

"ALL THINGS COME OF THEE, O LORD"

Reading what has been written about payment for spiritual direction, I noticed that, aside from the occasional mention of fees charged for services such as massages or piano lessons, the basis for comparison was almost always one of the mental health professions. That is, discussions about fees most often proceeded along the lines of "What is valued when we accept $75 fees for counseling but question $40 fees for spiritual direction?"[15] Such questions were then followed by theories (or complaints) about why the going rate for one was so much higher than for the other.

But could not an equally valid point be made by looking in a different direction for a reference group? That is, what about the unpaid services provided by vocational deacons, sponsors in twelve-step recovery programs, and the multitudes of churchgoers who offer their time to help keep their parishes operating? Or what about people who volunteer their assistance to hospitals, literacy programs, Boy Scout or Girl Scout troops, or countless other community organizations? What about members of service clubs, such as Rotary or Lions? What about businesses and law firms that do some pro bono work? Even the American Psychoanalytic Association, which I had once stereotyped as being solidly representative of fee-for-service thinking, stated in the social responsibility section of its latest code of ethics that "a psychoanalyst is encouraged to contribute a portion of his or her time and talents to activities that serve the interests of patients and the public good."[16]

TIME AND TALENTS

My own tendency at this point is to regard my offering of spiritual direction *as an offering*, as an expression of stewardship. For some reason I am not comfortable about giving my time and talents only in exchange for treasure. Although I am happy to receive a stipend from an organization or a fee or other compensation for conducting a workshop or retreat, particularly when I incur expenses, I do not accept payment from individuals. I suppose I aspire to be an "amateur" in the sense that Margaret Guenther defined the term: "one who loves, loves the art that she serves, loves and prays for the people who trust her, loves the Holy Spirit who is the true director in this strange ministry called spiritual direction."[17] I cherish a T-shirt created for me by two Jewish friends when I made a substantial reduction in my work hours to allow more time for spiritual direction. It reads, "I do it for the *mitzvah*!"[18]

How do I deal with the possibility that directees will feel guilty or "one-down" if they don't pay me a fee? Most of those I have encountered so far contribute or have contributed some of their own time and talents to church and/or community. Several of them, in fact, regularly volunteer more hours per month than I do. When I inform prospective directees during our initial meeting that I will not charge them a fee or expect any other form of payment, I also ask them whether they are paid for teaching Sunday school, singing in the choir, leading the youth group, attending vestry meetings, organizing the church fair, making calls for the stewardship campaign, working at the food pantry, transporting patients in the nursing home, or cooking for the homeless shelter. When I put my offering of spiritual direction in the same category as the unpaid services they perform, the parallel is clear. Those not involved in volunteer work likewise do not seem to have difficulty with the concept (and often find themselves drawn toward volunteering as direction proceeds).

Likening my offering of spiritual direction to directees' own activities may help reduce their discomfort about "getting something for nothing." Perhaps it even serves to deprofessionalize my role and put us on a more equal footing. What I do ask from directees in exchange is that they be respectful of my time; that is, do their best to arrive for meetings on time and give reasonable notice about cancellations or schedule changes. Occasionally directees have brought me small gifts related in some way to our work together (e.g., books or devotional items) or made donations in my honor to charitable organizations.

Would I have more time and energy available to do more spiritual direction if I didn't also have to work at a job that pays? Definitely. If a parish or other organization offers me a stipend to conduct spiritual direction in that setting, do I accept it? Yes. Do I feel comfortable about asking directees themselves to pay me? No. Will my answers to these three questions remain the same forever? Who knows? At present, my decisions on this issue are based on the belief that direct payment, whether for time or for "expertise," alters to some degree the interpersonal dynamics of the relationship. For me, if not for the directee, such an arrangement would likely foster a subtle expectation to "produce," to get "results," no matter how firmly I believe that God is the real director. For me, if not for the directee, that expectation would be disruptive. But I acknowledge that my decisions about payment are mine alone, based at least as much on my own personal dynamics as on objective considerations, and I respect those who have arrived at other solutions to this complex question for which there is no clear answer.

Notes

1. Robert J. Willis, "Professionalism, Legal Responsibilities and Record Keeping," *Presence* 1:1 (January 1995), 42–43.

2. Ibid., 41.

3. For example, Elizabeth G. Stout, "Building Your Practice of Spiritual Direction," *Presence* 7:1 (January 2001), 29–39.

4. Peter Ball, *Anglican Spiritual Direction* (Cambridge, MA: Cowley Publications, 1998), 187.

5. Garth Kasimu Baker-Fletcher, "Just Boundaries or Mean-Spirited Surveillance?" in *Boundary Wars: Intimacy and Distance in Healing Relationships*, ed. Katherine Hancock Ragsdale (Cleveland: Pilgrim Press, 1996), 141.

6. Karen Lebacqz and Joseph D. Driskill, *Ethics and Spiritual Care: A Guide for Pastors, Chaplains, and Spiritual Directors* (Nashville: Abingdon Press, 2000), 82.

7. Ball, *Anglican Spiritual Direction*, 187.

8. Bill Creed, "Dignity and Worth: The Question of Compensation for Spiritual Direction," *Presence* 1:3 (September 1995), 45.

9. Ibid., 46.

10. Ibid.

11. Jonathan Foster, "Liability Issues in a Ministry of Spiritual Direction," *Presence* 2:3 (September 1996), 53.

12. Richard S. Epstein, *Keeping Boundaries: Maintaining Safety and Integrity in the Psychotherapeutic Process* (Washington, DC: American Psychiatric Press, 1994), 173. See Chapter 4 in this book for additional discussion.

13. Lebacqz and Driskill, *Ethics and Spiritual Care*, 82.

14. Creed, "Dignity and Worth," 49.

15. Ibid., 48.

16. American Psychoanalytic Association, *Principles and Standards of Ethics for Psychoanalysts*, http://www.apsa.org/ethics901.htm, revised September 24, 2001.

17. Margaret Guenther, *Holy Listening: The Art of Spiritual Direction* (Cambridge, MA: Cowley Publications, 1992), 1.

18. *Mitzvah* means commandment; commonly, a "good work" or act of charity in accord with God's will.

~

CHAPTER FOUR

Dual Relationships

PAULETTE, QUEENA, AND RONALD: *Paulette is a priest who works in an administrative position at a church-related organization. Recently she began offering spiritual direction on weekends. Her first directee, Queena, mentioned that her husband, Ronald, was also interested in receiving direction and said she thought Paulette would be the ideal director for him as well. Because she was interested in having more directees and testing out some insights from a pastoral theology course she took on family systems, Paulette agreed to meet with both individually.*

But now, after only a few meetings, she realizes she is beginning to dread seeing either of them. Each spouse seems to be trying to use the spiritual direction discussions to validate religious opinions that differ from the other's, and Paulette finds herself mentally siding with Queena on so many issues that her conversations with Ronald are becoming awkward. On the morning of her next appointment with him, she develops a severe migraine headache and has to reschedule.

SAMUEL AND TRUDY: *Samuel is a seminarian doing his field placement at a small suburban parish. He is intensely interested in spirituality and began offering spiritual direction in-*

formally before entering the ordination process. Now several members of the congregation have approached him to discuss spiritual issues. Because there are no other directors available in or anywhere near the community, he has agreed to see them.

At tonight's vestry meeting he notices that Trudy, an older member of the congregation who told him some unusually intimate things about her life during their spiritual direction session last week, seems to be avoiding eye contact with him. When the vestry meeting ends she glances at him, looks away, and hurries out of the room. Samuel wonders whether she might be feeling awkward about seeing him in this context after what she shared with him.

BROTHER ULRIC AND VICTOR: *For many years Brother Ulric has been offering spiritual direction as one of his principal responsibilities at the monastery. Victor is a medical doctor who has been one of his directees for almost a decade. Over the years their relationship has become more informal. They meet for dinner whenever Brother Ulric comes to conduct a program in the town where Victor lives, and Brother Ulric sometimes asks Victor for advice about his or the other monks' medical concerns. Although their relationship includes a considerable amount of mutuality these days, Brother Ulric still makes a point of focusing their discussion on his directee's issues whenever they meet for spiritual direction.*

~

Dual relationships, or multiple roles, are defined as situations in which a director and directee regularly have other dealings or connections with each other outside their spiritual direction meetings. Some examples are:

- directing one's own family member, friend, colleague, student, or supervisee;
- directing a current directee's family member or close friend;

- working closely or frequently with a directee in parish or community activities;
- socializing with a directee;
- having a business relationship with a directee;
- bartering or exchanging services with a directee.[1]

Spiritual direction is, by its very nature, a relationship of unusual intimacy and trust. It is not even simply a two-way connection: rather, it involves the relationship of the directee to God *and* that of the director to God *as well as* the relationship of the directee to the director. The question of whether dual relationships ought to be prohibited or to what extent they are acceptable is complicated enough for the helping professions these days; it is even more complicated for spiritual direction because of the unusual nature of this relationship.

DUAL RELATIONSHIPS: NO?

What is it about spiritual direction that makes this issue so challenging? While I was preparing this chapter, a friend of mine who is a piano teacher as well as a spiritual director told me about an experience she had just had at the home of one of her students. After the piano lesson the girl's parents had invited her to stay for dinner, and the visit had been extremely pleasant. In her role as a piano teacher, the appropriateness of spending a social evening with the student and her family was not an issue that my friend had to weigh for very long; if one of her directees had invited her to dinner, however, it certainly would have been.

What is wrong with being involved in dual relationships with directees? Arguments for avoiding relationship overlap whenever possible usually center on the questions of conflict, confidentiality, transference, and potential for harm. Spiritual direction meetings are presumably more intimate than music lessons. Directees need to feel that they can safely tell us things they have never discussed with anyone else, or things about which they feel ashamed or "not okay." The sharing of sensitive information has the potential to arouse feelings on both sides that must be handled with great care and respect, especially in small communities.

Those who favor restricting dual relationships emphasize the importance of offering the directee as uncluttered an interpersonal space as possible for the process of direction to unfold. *A Code of Ethics for Spiritual Directors* states: "The primary goal is to ensure a 'clean' space for spiritual direction, while still allowing the Spirit to move freely; the touchstone is that any mixing of roles not compromise the effectiveness of the spiritual direction relationship."

As Linda Julian of the Order of St. Helena explained: "In order to maintain good boundaries, one needs to choose a director who is not a personal friend of any kind, especially anyone in one's immediate faith community. . . . Your spiritual director needs to be someone whom you don't regularly meet in other contexts and with whom you don't share a lot of other relationships."[2] In other words, the less additional "baggage" there is in the relationship, the more freely it can move.

A potential source of difficulty in any relationship is transference. Transference, a concept which originated in psychoanalytic theory, is the tendency of all human beings to bring to their interactions certain emotional reactions and needs from their past, most often in connection with parents and other early family members, with resulting distortion of a present relationship. Some degree of transference is present in all human relating; the point at which it becomes a problem is when one person feels or behaves toward another as if that person were someone else. In spiritual direction, manifestations of transference might include feeling unduly angry at or attracted to the director; being preoccupied with impressing the director; attributing extraordinary powers to the director; or responding rebelliously or submissively in the direction relationship when such responses do not fit the situation.

With respect to dual relationships, transference can be a cause for concern if the directee's feelings about the director unduly influence how he or she behaves in other settings (e.g., on a parish committee), make the directee vulnerable to exploitation, or otherwise interfere with making appropriate choices. For instance, transference might be a factor if Ronald were to find himself inclined to oppose everything Paulette said without much reflection, or if Queena were to look constantly to Paulette for validation instead of trying to think things out for herself. Likewise, transference might be implicated if Trudy were excessively worried about what Samuel thought of her, or if Victor didn't really want to socialize with Brother Ulric or didn't want to discuss his medical problems, but acquiesced in order to avoid risking his director's disapproval. An outstanding discussion of transference dynamics and their ethical implications in the context of spiritual direction can be found in Janet K. Ruffing's *Spiritual Direction: Beyond the Beginnings* in the chapter "The 'As If' Relationship: Transference and Countertransference in Spiritual Direction."

Some who think dual relationships should be restricted or prohibited have cited research on psychotherapy which suggests that involvement in such relationships may be a prelude to clearly inappropriate transgressions of personal boundaries, such as sexual misconduct.[3] The theory behind this so-called slippery slope phenomenon is that the crossing of one boundary without adverse consequences increases the likelihood that another will be crossed, and so on. However, this supposition has been the object of considerable dispute among therapy practitioners and researchers.[4]

DUAL RELATIONSHIPS: YES?

Arguments in favor of openness with respect to overlapping relationships often point out that spiritual direction is more egalitarian than psychotherapy, has less frequent meetings, is less dependent on the director's own skills, and involves not only two human beings but also God. Indeed, even *A Code of Ethics for Spiritual Directors* notes that the direction relationship "has a three-way nature which includes a God with a long history of breaking rules!" Proponents of relatively more flexibility in such relationships cau-

tion against the indiscriminate borrowing of assumptions and practices from the literature on psychotherapy and assert that "hard and
fast statements that urge a director to avoid every occasion where
dual/multiple relationships might result do not leave sufficient room
for the often surprising movements of the holy."[5]

Indeed, the reality is that it is difficult, if not impossible, to
avoid some multiplicity of relationships in many religious settings.
Pastors of congregations regularly interact with parishioners in the
work of the church and in their neighborhoods. The smaller the
community, the greater the chances for overlap. In rural areas, mil-
itary settings, or ethnic or lesbian and gay communities where just
about everybody knows just about everybody else, it may be virtually impossible to avoid multiple relationships.[6]

Some arguments on the positive side of the question are cen-
tered on the sociopolitics of inequality. For those who propose
such arguments, the term *boundaries* tends to imply exclusion, hi-
erarchy, overcontrol, or lack of genuine caring. The feminist therapist Miriam Greenspan, for example, commented critically on
what she termed the "distance model" that is "the reigning psy-
chodynamic paradigm of psychotherapy" in our culture.[7] Citing
Greenspan's work, the spiritual director Sandra Lommasson
Pickens opposed the borrowing for spiritual direction of this
model in which "the only safe connection is one bounded by distance from the rest of life. For some, this translates into a nar-
rowly defined rule that one does not see or encounter directees
outside of the direction session."[8] She continued: "I have to
wonder how much of this model . . . is distinctly American with
its focus on the individual and the attempt to manage life through
carving it up into distinct compartments."[9]

If our ideas about interpersonal boundaries are grounded in
prevailing cultural norms and tend to produce an unnatural com-
partmentalization of experience, awareness of cultural differences
may suggest other ways of thinking about dual relationships.[10] For
example, the pastor Mari E. Castellanos wrote of the Hispanic
community in which she grew up: "The priest who baptized me,

married my parents, and buried my grandparents, was a good friend of the family. Both he and my parents would have found any criticism of this dual relationship highly offensive. Our family physicians, a husband-and-wife team, were also close friends of my parents, regarded as family. Any implication that this could be construed as unethical or inappropriate would be so ludicrous to them and to my parents that it would simply be dismissed immediately."[11] She went on to offer the excellent suggestion that "it is essential that we demythologize the roles of certain professionals. Pastors, physicians, and therapists are not gods, but rather professionals with a limited field of expertise, like engineers and accountants. Bringing pulpits down to pew level will go a long way toward eliminating abuse."[12]

So?

The question of the appropriateness of dual relationships in spiritual direction is one for which there is no single, generally applicable answer. Those who think that dual relationships should be permissible offer the valid argument that transference plays a more significant role in therapy than it does in spiritual direction, in which the relationship with God rather than the relationship with the director is seen as the principal agent of change. Nevertheless, it is important to remember that transference is present in all relationships. The fact that it is not employed as a vehicle for change does not negate its potential to cause problems in any given situation.

Existing codes of ethics and guidelines for spiritual direction acknowledge the challenges and risks posed by dual relationships, but they do not automatically prohibit them. In the final analysis, the answer to what to do about a particular case of relationship overlap may well boil down to "it depends." Certainly such relationships should be entered into only with a great deal of care, honest mutual reflection, and clarity about purposes and alternatives. The most important concern may be not whether relationships are "dual" but rather whether they are nonsexual, nonexploitative, and nonharmful—and that such relationships never benefit the director to the detriment of any directee.

For directors and directees who find themselves in dual relationships, deliberate and ongoing evaluation by all parties is essential. An especially important question is whether the overlap distorts, or may distort, the relationship. It appears that Paulette is becoming a pawn in her directees' battle of theologies. Queena seems to be trying to use direction to shore up her own religious arguments rather than to pursue spiritual growth, and her husband, Ronald, is getting shortchanged by their director's responses to Queena's opinions. Paulette's decision to enter into such an arrangement may well have been inadvisable. But now that the arrangement exists, can she identify and confront the problem squarely with each member of the couple? Is there any possibility that she can help them learn to use spiritual direction as a space for exploration rather than a source of ammunition? Can she listen to each of them with the degree of objectivity to which every directee is entitled? Would meeting with them together rather than separately be a helpful modification? Or have both of these direction relationships been so compromised by what has already taken place that referral of Queena and Ronald to other directors would be the best way to achieve a "clean space" for everyone concerned?

Samuel, the seminarian, ought to have anticipated the potential for discomfort for directees whom he would also encounter in other parish activities, and he should have discussed this possibility with Trudy at the outset of their spiritual direction arrangement. In any event, he should initiate a straightforward conversation about the vestry meeting incident at the outset of their next direction appointment. Was Trudy's behavior at the meeting indeed caused by embarrassment about what she had told Samuel the last time they met for spiritual direction? If so, what are her concerns? Is she worried about what he thinks of her now and/or about how he might handle the information? How can she be assured that nothing she tells him will be shared or used to her detriment? And Samuel should ask himself how he feels toward Trudy at this point. Is there anything about what she told him (e.g., similarity to a significant problem he or someone close to him is having) that might affect his work with her? How can he best reflect God's love and acceptance to her now? If she continues to feel uncomfortable about seeing him at parish meetings, what might they do about that? If she is reluctant to share with Samuel sensitive information about herself in the future, what might they do about that?

Victor and Brother Ulric would likely benefit from periodic, frank discussions of the state of their relationship. How does the increasing mutuality affect the ability of either of them to be honest with the other, to raise problems and tell hard truths? Is there enough edge left in the relationship for it to be challenging and spiritually growth-producing for Victor, or has it become so relaxed and familiar that he doesn't get as much out of it as he once did? How does Victor really feel about Brother Ulric's discussing his medical concerns with him? Most important of all, what needs of his own might Brother Ulric be indulging in their current relationship, and is it sufficient that he tries to set aside his own interests and issues for the hour that they define as spiritual direction? It is Brother Ulric's responsibility to see that Victor continues to benefit from spiritual direction with him and to enable him to move on to another director if their direction relationship has run its course.

Notes

1. Adapted from Thomas M. Hedberg, Betsy Caprio, and the Staff of the Center for Sacred Psychology, *A Code of Ethics for Spiritual Directors*, rev. ed. (Pecos, NM: Dove Publications, 1992), 8.

2. Linda Julian, "On Finding a Spiritual Director," *Quarterly Newsletter of the Order of St. Helena* 20:1 (March 1999), 1; available at http://www.osh.org/ministries/Ministries(LJarticle).

3. For instance, Richard S. Epstein, *Keeping Boundaries: Maintaining Safety and Integrity in the Psychotherapeutic Process* (Washington, DC: American Psychiatric Press, 1994), 173; Jerry Edelwich and Archie

Brodsky, *Sexual Dilemmas for the Helping Professional*, rev. ed. (New York: Brunner/Mazel, 1991), 139; and Glen O. Gabbard and Eva P. Lester, *Boundaries and Boundary Violations in Psychoanalysis* (New York: Basic Books, 1996).

4. For instance, Ofer Zur, "Out-of-Office Experience: When Crossing Office Boundaries and Engaging in Dual Relationships are Clinically Beneficial and Ethically Sound," *Independent Practitioner* 21:1 (Spring 2001), 96-100; available at http://www.drzur.com/outofoffice.html.

5. Sandra Lommasson Pickens, "Looking at Dual/Multiple Relationships: Danger or Opportunity?", *Presence* 2:2 (May 1996), 53.

6. Mari E. Castellanos, "Barriers Not Withstanding: A Lesbianista Perspective," in *Boundary Wars: Intimacy and Distance in Healing Relationships*, ed. Katherine Hancock Ragsdale (Cleveland: Pilgrim Press, 1996), 200; Zur, "Out-of-Office Experience."

7. Miriam Greenspan, "Out of Bounds," in *Boundary Wars*, 131.

8. Lommasson Pickens, "Looking at Dual/Multiple Relationships," 53–54.

9. Ibid., 54.

10. Leng Leroy Lim, "Exploring Embodiment," in *Boundary Wars*, 58–77; Margo Rivera, "I-Thou: Interpersonal Boundaries in the Therapy Relationship," in *Boundary Wars*, 194; Castellanos, "Barriers Not Withstanding,"197–207; and Sherlon Brown and Carmen Williams, "To Discriminate or Not to Discriminate: Culture and Ethics," *Counseling Today* (April 2000), 16f.

11. Castellanos, "Barriers Not Withstanding," 199.

12. Ibid., 200.

~

CHAPTER FIVE

Attraction

WALTER AND XIAO-YING: *Walter is a vocational deacon assigned by his diocese to a large urban parish. His responsibilities include offering spiritual direction. One of his directees, Xiao-Ying, is a woman in her early thirties who has recently transferred from another church for reasons she has not yet managed to articulate to him, although he has noticed that she talks a lot about her former rector. Lately she has begun sending Walter several e-mails each day with quotations from scripture, comments about books she has read, or reactions to the previous week's sermon. Already in a committed relationship, he is beginning to feel a bit uncomfortable about what all this attention might mean. He decides to try to express this feeling to Xiao-Ying during their next meeting, but just as he is starting to do so, she declares that she loves him and quietly begins to cry.*

YVES AND ZULEIKA: *Yves is a former monk who left his religious order to marry a former nun. He now teaches philosophy at a church-affiliated college and offers spiritual direction at a retreat center. Several months ago, to his dismay, his wife told him that she needed some time alone to "think things through" and moved out.*

He has been assigned to meet with Zuleika, who has come

to the center for a seven-day directed retreat. On the second day of her retreat, Zuleika tells him that her fiancé, whom she had been dating since college, broke their engagement only two weeks before their wedding and is now planning to marry another woman. She says that since this happened she has felt utterly unattractive, unwanted, and rejected, even by God. As Yves listens, he suddenly finds himself wondering whether her stalled prayer life might be helped if he were to tell her how deeply and personally he can understand her feelings and per-haps even offer her some reassurance of her desirability.

ALEXANDRA AND BOB: *Alexandra is a divorcée in her fifties who offers spiritual direction at her church on Sundays. Her newest directee, Bob, is a tall, powerful-looking man who recently turned forty. During her second meeting with him, she finds she is fascinated by his decidedly "masculine" approach to spirituality. As he reflects on the day's gospel reading about Jesus and Mary Magdalene, she loses track of time, and their conversation goes on for at least half an hour longer than scheduled. At the end of the meeting, he tells her how much he appreciated the intense quality of her listening and then mum-bles something about how his wife usually seems a lot less in-terested in what he says. Hearing this, Alexandra realizes that it has been some time since a man, especially one like Bob, complimented her.*

⌒

Kenneth Leech put it succinctly: "Spirituality and sexuality are in-separable."[1] We are embodied persons, and it would be neither pos-sible nor desirable for us to separate our sexual feelings from the rest of life. "Spirituality has come to be seen by some as the rejec-tion of the body," Leech continued. "An essential part of spiritual direction is the healing of wounds caused by [the Western Christian history of regarding sexuality as evil] and other distorted views, and helping individuals to see the unity of sexual and spiritual life."[2]

A tall order. In her outstanding discussion of love mysticism in spiritual direction, Janet K. Ruffing noted that "our desires energize the spiritual quest and lead us to God" and that "our desires, our wants, our longings, our outward and inward searching—when uncovered, expressed and recognized—all lead to the Divine Beloved at the core."[3] If sexual passion and spiritual passion are manifestations of the same energy and are central to the spiritual search, how, in practical terms, are we to sort out and deal with such powerful feelings in ourselves and our directees?

The spiritual direction setting invites intense emotions, some of which may feel unusual. "Where else, and how often, can you find a place in which you are invited to talk freely and at length, without inhibitions, about your own personal journey?" asked Linda Julian in describing what to expect in the direction relationship. "Most of us have a need—indeed, a longing—for this, but we are not always able to find the appropriate place to get this very urgent need met."[4]

The psychiatrist and spiritual director Gerald G. May commented, "It has long been noted that the process of spiritual awakening and growth is associated with periods of rising sexual passion. . . . Often these energies surface as passionate feelings that seem to be looking for an object. It is all well and good to say that their true object is God, but pilgrims who find themselves suddenly infused with passion may have difficulty seeing God as a sufficiently identifiable, immediate, and substantial object."[5]

What's the Problem?

If a person comes to spiritual direction in search of a closer relationship with the Divine Beloved and ends up in a sexual relationship with the human being from whom he or she sought assistance, what are the implications? How does such a situation differ from any other interaction between consenting adults? The problem is that one longing can easily be confused with another, and such circumstances can set the scene for exploitation or other problematic conduct.

One of the virtually universal elements in codes of ethics for helping professions and other healing relationships is a prohibition against sexual intimacy with current patients, clients, or directees. This prohibition is a response to the potential for harm that can arise from the power differential and transference potential inherent in such relationships, as well as the disruption such involvement can cause for the helping relationship as originally constituted.

Definitions of inappropriate conduct have been more and more specifically and prolifically delineated in recent years, and official policies concerning it have become increasingly stringent. According to one Episcopal diocese's statement of policy, for example, sexual behavior is defined as "any kind of behavior that is designed to give sexual gratification to any of the parties involved," and "sexual misconduct occurs whenever one person violates his or her position by using or manipulating another for his or her own sexual gratification."[6] In spelling out its stance on sexual misconduct, the diocese "forbids all members of the clergy and all lay church workers from engaging in, or trying to engage in, sexual behavior . . . with a person . . . who is under the professional care of the member of the clergy or lay church worker in any way."[7] Likewise, another Episcopal diocese defines sexual exploitation as "the development of or the attempt to develop a sexual relationship between a cleric, employee, or volunteer and a person with whom s/he has a pastoral and/or fiduciary relationship, whether or not there is apparent consent from the individual."[8] Both policies also specify that these rules apply to spiritual directors, regardless of whether they are lay or ordained, paid or volunteer.

Not everyone views this trend toward more explicit definitions and stricter regulations as a positive development. Some have argued that these measures go too far or tend to reinforce patriarchal power differentials that are patronizing to adults, especially women. Other criticisms are that such sanctions might be applied disproportionately against gay, lesbian, unmarried, or controversial clergy, or seem more likely to protect institutions than individuals, or are "driven by obsessive fear of litigation and public censure."[9] Some have pointed out that current regulations can become barriers to the climate of closeness and mutuality that churches have traditionally offered.[10] Others object that they substitute simplistic rule-making for complex analysis;[11] reduce the likelihood that pastoral caregivers who are having difficulties will feel safe to explore their problems honestly in supervision;[12] or "create an anonymous, automatic morality for which no one has to accept personal responsibility."[13] Noting that transference is ubiquitous, some in this field regard transference phenomena as providing opportunities for mutuality and transformative relationship enhancement, rather than as potential sources of difficulty that need to be regulated.[14]

It is true that spiritual direction is generally more egalitarian than therapy or counseling, and so perhaps boundaries between director and directee can under some circumstances be more flexible. However, most who have written about this topic tend to favor remaining on the side of caution.

MISCONDUCT AND EXPLOITATION

However it is defined, sexual misconduct by those in positions of influence has been the subject of countless books and articles over the past decade. A pioneering work was Peter Rutter's *Sex in the Forbidden Zone: When Men in Power—Therapists, Doctors, Clergy, Teachers, and Others—Betray Women's Trust*. Like several other early books in this field, Rutter's discussion is limited to depicting men as the exploiters and women as the exploited, seeming not to recognize that other gender configurations are possible and that the roles of victim and victimizer might be locations on a continuum rather than pure categories. Nevertheless, the points he made are important. He noted that "intimate relationships of trust are especially vulnerable to boundary abuse because they invite both men and women to pour into them their strongest hopes, wishes, fantasies, and passions."[15] Of particular value to this book is his explanation of how, by remaining focused on the original purpose of the relationship rather than allowing themselves to be seduced by troubled patients, helpers are uniquely positioned to facilitate the process of healing.

Indeed, many people, particularly survivors of childhood sexual abuse, may act in seductive ways toward those they see as authority figures. They may be reenacting past abusive interactions or acting out of a belief that their sexuality is all they have to offer. What these individuals need most urgently in such situations is a response that does *not* repeat the past and revictimize them. "If a parishioner acts out sexually, the minister should recognise it as a clear cry for help," stated Pamela Cooper-White concerning pastoral sexual abuse. "The pastoral relationship can and should be a sacred trust, a place where a parishioner can come with the deepest wounds and vulnerabilities—where she can even act out sexually. By modeling appropriate boundaries and healthy responses, the pastor can begin to empower her to heal those wounds."[16] By relating to such a person as a whole human being worthy to be respected, rather than a sexual object ready to be used, the pastor or director can be of great help to her in the process of changing her damaged view of herself.

Abuse of a relationship of trust can have extremely harmful consequences for the mental, physical, and spiritual health of individuals, their families, and even entire congregations or communities. In *Is Nothing Sacred: When Sex Invades the Pastoral Relationship*, for example, Marie M. Fortune detailed a particularly appalling real-life example of multiple abuse of congregants and colleagues by an evidently sociopathic minister. But many instances of misconduct or exploitation involve not obvious, habitual sexual predators but rather ordinary, flawed humans not unlike the rest of us, who find themselves in situations where it is all too easy to become "unhealed wounders."[17]

Another damaging concomitant of sexual misconduct is its

potential to interfere with the client's or directee's access to the type of help she or he originally sought. Of sexual contact between clinicians and their clients, the mental-health trainers and researchers Jerry Edelwich and Archie Brodsky suggested that "however the client may feel at the time of the sexual involvement, the uneasiness that almost invariably follows not only removes the therapist/lover as a source of support in the future, but also makes it more difficult for the client to trust any therapist."[18] At the very least, when a relationship that begins as spiritual direction turns into a sexual liaison, it ceases to be spiritual direction.

Unfortunately, sexual misconduct seems to be a type of boundary problem which is somewhat resistant to institutional solutions. So-called zero-tolerance policies may well limit the extent to which individuals and organizations can sidestep, cover up, or explain away accusations of abuse, and such policies certainly help the policy makers feel that they have done something drastic and definitive. Nevertheless, the fact remains that elaborate codes of ethics and guidelines for conduct have been drawn up, adopted, and periodically updated for virtually all helping professions, yet many who are intent on misbehaving still proceed as if such guidelines did not exist. As the pastor Mari E. Castellanos put it, "It is not the absence of boundaries that has made clergy abuse of parishioners possible. A priest who has sexual relations with an altar boy is not drawn to it by any lack of boundaries. The book is full of rules against it; he just chose to break them."[19]

Personal therapy and extensive self-knowledge on the part of the helper are important safeguards against misconduct. However, even these provide no guarantee that helpers will always behave appropriately. As the psychiatry professors Glen Gabbard and Eva Lester noted in discussing ethical violations by psychoanalysts, "Although we would like to think that a thorough personal analysis is prophylactic for vulnerability to transgressions such as analyst-patient sex, experience suggests otherwise."[20] These authors detailed an astonishing array of rationalizations and self-deceptions used by transgressors to justify their conduct to themselves and others. Most often, the transgressors either considered themselves above such "ordinary" rules or convinced themselves that their actions were intended only for their patients' benefit.

It is important to keep in mind that the responsibility for making appropriate decisions in helping relationships belongs to the designated helpers. Writing about women and pastoral abuse, Pamela Cooper-White pointed out that "even if a woman initiated the sexual contact out of her own need or vulnerability, the pastor, like a therapist, has the responsibility to maintain the appropriate boundary."[21] Trying to blame our behavior on the directee or client ("She was just too attractive"/ "He was out to seduce me"/ "She caught me at a weak moment") is simply not an acceptable response to our own poor judgment.

In situations which present opportunities for sexual exploitation, clear thinking and commitment to ethical conduct by the helper are crucial. Decisions about what, exactly, constitutes appropriate behavior should be made *before* we find ourselves in tempting situations. Wavering in response to a sexual invitation by a directee, for example, can ultimately do more damage than a matter-of-fact refusal.[22]

Walter's response to Xiao-Ying's declaration of love should reflect sensitivity to her feelings while communicating unambiguously his intention not to relate to her in a romantic or sexual way. The manner in which he does this is important. Responses such as "I'm attracted to you, too, but there are rules against getting involved with parishioners" or "Sorry, but I'm in a committed relationship right now" might well result in her thinking she has reason to hope for a different response at some point in the future. Likewise, if he were to say something like "Sorry, but I'm gay," he would be failing to make the point that sexual involvement is not consistent with the nature of the spiritual direction relationship in any case. Instead, he might acknowledge the feelings she has expressed and move them into the context of the original purpose of the relationship, beginning with something like "Remember, we agreed at the outset that a romantic relationship is not what you and I are here for. But I think that what you're feeling is very important. Can we talk about how I might help you *as your spiritual director*?" Because Xiao-Ying's behavior may reflect a history of abuse (perhaps even by clergy), he might also start preparing to offer her a therapy referral, taking care to do so in such a way that she will not feel hurt or rejected—and to direct her to a therapist who can be trusted to deal appropriately with her vulnerability in this area.

Yves might find it easy to convince himself that his intense personal response to Zuleika's feelings of rejection is a positive development and that she would benefit from knowing that she is attractive in his eyes. But how reliable is his instant assumption that he knows exactly how she feels, and would being told that she is attractive really help resolve the problems in her prayer life? Would either of them be better off if a rebound romance were to develop between them in the context of an intensive residential retreat? Instead, Yves's likely overidentification with Zuleika should serve as a signal to him that he needs to back off and consider how his own issues may be coming into play. And he certainly ought to remind himself of the reason she came to him in the first place. As a spiritual director, Yves is probably the person in his directee's life who is best qualified to help her explore the urgent question of where God is for her in her painful circumstances.

TEMPTATION AND DISTRACTION

Not all situations with potential for interpersonal boundary problems resemble the pairing of Little Red Riding Hood and the Big Bad Wolf, with a predatory man in a position of power over a vulnerable woman. In the case of Alexandra and Bob, the directee is a man, perhaps with some problems in his marriage and evidently with a need to be heard, and the director is a woman older than he, with a divorce in her history and missing the company of men. We could say that each of them, unconsciously or consciously, may be behaving in ways that the other might find seductive—Alexandra with her fascinated attention and disregard for time boundaries, and Bob with his implication that she is a better listener than his wife and perhaps with elements of his discussion of Mary Magdalene. We could also say that both of them are vulnerable. It is important to remember that we are all wounded and subject to being hurt and that there are irrational forces in all of us. Just because a situation does not look like a stereotypical scenario for exploitation does not mean there is no potential for difficulty.

Even if it doesn't lead to sexual involvement, strong attraction in the spiritual direction relationship can be distracting and disruptive. As Janet Ruffing noted about transference, "When the relationship between the director and directee—instead of the directee's relationship with God—becomes . . . a preoccupation for the directee, the entire process of spiritual direction can be sidetracked."[23] Likewise, a director's responses to a directee who thinks she or he is superhumanly wonderful can distort or interfere with the work at hand. In a book addressed to helping professionals, a male psychologist was quoted as admitting that "In my first few years on the job I would keep coming back to female patients whose transference took the form of adoration of me. It's hard not to give extra attention to someone who idealizes you."[24] And, as Ruffing noted, "if we begin to believe the flattery of our directees, we may more easily become careless about boundary issues."[25]

It is clearly Alexandra's responsibility to see that appropriate boundaries between her and Bob are maintained. Presumably Bob came to spiritual direction in search of a closer relationship with God, not an extramarital sexual adventure with his director. Presumably Alexandra is capable of addressing her own needs in contexts other than her relationships with directees. If she were to have ongoing difficulty functioning within the customary parameters of spiritual direction with this directee, she would be well advised to follow recommendations offered to mental health professionals and clergy who find themselves attracted to those they have set out to help, namely:

- Acknowledge the feelings to yourself honestly, rather than trying to deny or explain away the attraction.
- Remember the difference between feelings and behavior—that is, resolve to speak and behave appropriately no matter how you may feel at the moment.
- Mentally subject your present and future behavior with this directee to a "publicity test": If other people were to see or hear about what you were doing or thinking of doing, would they think it was appropriate?
- Ask yourself what there might be about this person that engages one or several of your own needs.
- Seek supervision or discuss the situation frankly with a trusted, experienced colleague.
- Consider seeking therapy to work on your unresolved issues.
- If you are unable to resolve or manage your feelings appropriately, terminate the relationship (with great care!) and help the directee find another director.[26]

CONCLUSIONS AND SUGGESTIONS

Karen Lebacqz and Joseph D. Driskill have pointed out that spiritual direction differs from pastoral counseling or psychotherapy in the sense that "spiritual direction sessions are not to the same degree a ministry to the hurting or vulnerable (although people in direction can be dealing with hurts and be vulnerable)."[27] They noted that the relative infrequency of meetings, the emphasis on growth rather than on resolving dysfunction, and the greater responsibility placed on the directee—in addition to the fact that in spiritual direction the object of such feelings is supposed to be God, not the human director—usually serve to minimize transference attachments to the director.

Nevertheless, the potential for attraction in the spiritual direction relationship does exist, and it needs to be acknowledged and handled with care. Because spiritual direction so often involves searching and reaching for the numinous, it is not altogether surprising that "directees sometimes weave the director right into their relationship with God."[28] The first step in managing the potential for attraction is for directors to do all they can to enhance their own health in this area. Kenneth Leech said, "The spiritual director must be a person who is facing his own sexuality and sexual needs, a person who is on the way towards sexual integrity and wholeness."[29] Another step is to work out boundaries or ground rules which are clearly defined and understood by all parties at the outset. Such boundaries help minimize problems and misunderstandings. To borrow once again from the psychoanalytic literature, "Boundaries define the parameters of the analytic relationship so that both patient and analyst can be safe while also being spontaneous. . . . The analytic frame creates an atmosphere of *safety*. . . . It is precisely because the rules of the game are different from all other social interactions that the patient is free to experience him- or herself in a new light."[30]

Applied in practical terms to spiritual direction, the boundary elements might include these:

- Making sure from the beginning of the relationship that all parties understand where boundaries will be set
- Limiting physical contact
- Limiting contact between meetings
- Forgoing most or all social contact
- Holding to the agreed-upon time frame
- Encouraging the directee's independence
- Remembering that the focus of direction is on God

If these boundary elements are defined and explicitly agreed upon at the outset of a spiritual direction relationship, the likelihood is greatly reduced that directees will take offense or feel hurt when reminded of them along the way. As Lebacqz and Driskill put it, "It is often better to err on the side of restraint by maintaining clear boundaries, than to chance blurring them out of a misguided or ill-conceived desire to be helpful."[31]

Notes

1. Kenneth Leech, *Soul Friend: A Study of Spirituality* (London: Sheldon Press, 1977), 115.

2. Ibid., 114.

3. Janet K. Ruffing, *Spiritual Direction: Beyond the Beginnings* (New York: Paulist Press, 2000), 9, 11.

4. Linda Julian, "On Finding a Spiritual Director," *Quarterly Newsletter of the Order of St. Helena* 20:1 (March 1999), 1; available at http://www.osh.org/ministries/Ministries(LJarticle).

5. Gerald G. May, *Care of Mind, Care of Spirit: A Psychiatrist Explores Spiritual Direction* (HarperSanFrancisco, 1992), 136.

6. Episcopal Diocese of New York, *Sexual Misconduct in the Church: What Are the Rules and How It is Handled*, http://www.dioceseny.org/convention/pbook/misconduct.html, accessed June 13, 2002.

7. Ibid.

8. Episcopal Diocese of Southern Ohio, *Policy and Definition of Sexual Misconduct*, http://www.episcopalian.org/dsoyouth/guide/paperwork/Misconduct.html, accessed June 13, 2002.

9. Carter Heyward and Beverly Wildung Harrison, "Boundaries: Protecting the Vulnerable or Perpetrating a Bad Idea?" in *Boundary Wars: Intimacy and Distance in Healing Relationships*, ed. Katherine Hancock Ragsdale (Cleveland: Pilgrim Press, 1996), 122, 124.

10. Fredrica Harris Thompsett, "Walking the Bounds: Historical and Theological Reflections on Ministry, Intimacy, and Power," in *Boundary Wars*, 36.

11. Margo Rivera, "I-Thou: Interpersonal Boundaries in the Therapy Relationship," in *Boundary Wars*, 186, 188.

12. Ibid., 192–193.

13. Ibid., 192.

14. Heyward and Harrison, "Boundaries," 116, 117–118.

15. Peter Rutter, *Sex in the Forbidden Zone* (Los Angeles: Jeremy P. Tarcher, 1989), 26.

16. Pamela Cooper-White, "Soul Stealing: Power Relations in Pastoral Sexual Abuse," *Christian Century Magazine* (February 20, 1991), http://www.anandainfo.com/soul_stealing.html.

17. Richard Irons and Katherine Roberts, "The Unhealed Wounders," in Nancy Myer Hopkins and Mark Laaser, eds., *Restoring the Soul of a Church: Healing Congregations Wounded by Clergy Sexual Misconduct* (Collegeville, MN: Liturgical Press, 1995), 33–51.

18. Jerry Edelwich and Archie Brodsky, *Sexual Dilemmas for the Helping Professional*, rev. ed. (New York: Brunner/Mazel, 1991), 68.

19. Mari E. Castellanos, "Barriers Not Withstanding: A *Lesbianista* Perspective," in *Boundary Wars*, 198.

20. Glen O. Gabbard and Eva P. Lester, *Boundaries and Boundary Violations in Psychoanalysis* (New York: Basic Books, 1996), 120.

21. Cooper-White, "Soul Stealing."

22. See Bill Wallace, "Care of the Dying: *Power Between, Power Under,* and *Powerlessness With* as Means for Valuing and Balancing Boundaries and Mutuality," in *Boundary Wars*, 212; and Karen Lebacqz and Ronald G. Barton, "Boundaries, Mutuality, and Professional Ethics," in *Boundary Wars*, 110, n. 30, for brief comments on this point.

23. Ruffing, *Spiritual Direction*, 162.

24. Edelwich and Brodsky, *Sexual Dilemmas*, 68.

25. Ruffing, *Spiritual Direction*, 171.

26. Adapted from Edelwich and Brodsky, *Sexual Dilemmas,* 120–138; Gerald Corey, Marianne Schneider Corey, and Patrick Callanan, *Issues and Ethics in the Helping Professions*, 4th ed. (Pacific Grove, CA: Brooks/Cole, 1993), 149; and Karen Lebacqz and Ronald G. Barton, *Sex in the Parish* (Louisville, KY: Westminster/John Knox Press, 1991), 42–67.

27. Karen Lebacqz and Joseph D. Driskill, *Ethics and Spiritual Care: A Guide for Pastors, Chaplains, and Spiritual Directors* (Nashville: Abingdon Press, 2000), 76.

28. Ruffing, *Spiritual Direction*, 171.

29. Leech, *Soul Friend*, 114.

30. Gabbard and Lester, *Boundaries and Boundary Violations*, 41.

31. Lebacqz and Driskill, *Ethics and Spiritual Care*, 74.

~

CHAPTER SIX

"Fixing Things"

CRAIG AND DENNIS: *Craig has been meeting regularly with his spiritual director, Dennis, a parish priest. Craig is a recovering alcoholic, and Dennis's mother died last year of alcohol-related cirrhosis. For the first two or three years of his recovery, Craig attended Alcoholics Anonymous meetings many times a week. Dennis attended some Al-Anon meetings for families and friends of alcoholics during the period preceding his mother's death but did not feel he had the time or energy to "work the steps." Lately, Craig has begun asking his director to lend him carfare to get home, and his breath has smelled of liquor. Knowing that he has no close relatives and few sources of support nearby, Dennis does not think he can just let his directee go "down the tubes" the way his mother did. He thinks he ought to confront him about his drinking and persuade him to stay at the rectory with his family until he has regained his sobriety.*

ESTHER AND SISTER FRANCES: *Esther is a childless widow in her early sixties with a moderately debilitating medical condition that does not seem to be improving despite several years of treatment by various specialists. She sees a psychologist once a week and a spiritual director once a month in an effort to deal with her feelings of despair and helplessness over this problem. Her spiritual director, Sister Frances, sometimes finds it difficult to listen to her reports of no improvement month after month but tries to remind herself that "fixing things" is the therapist's and the doctors' (and God's!) territory. When Esther arrives for their next meeting, she looks even more despondent than ever and announces that her health insurance coverage has been reduced and her coverage for therapy terminated. For the rest of the hour Sister Frances hears only parts of what her directee is saying, because she is so busy searching through her mental repertoire of possible solutions to the insurance problem.*

～

As spiritual directors and as human beings, we like to be helpful. It is satisfying to see people benefit from the assistance we offer them, and it can be distressing when we find ourselves unable to help someone. If we look a bit deeper into our experiences, motives, and rewards, we might find that helping another person can make us feel capable, connected, generous, special, powerful, and in control. Being unable to help another person can make us feel frustrated, incompetent, powerless, out of control, angry, and perhaps even guilty or blameworthy. But the inescapable reality is that sometimes we can help people, and sometimes we can't. Also, there are times when we should help people, and times when we shouldn't.

RESCUING

Rescuing is a term often used in connection with twelve-step recovery programs (groups for people with addictions and for their family members and friends) to describe inappropriate levels of caretaking. As Melody Beattie, a prominent author in this field, explained, "We rescue anytime we take responsibility for another human being—for that person's thoughts, feelings, decisions, behaviors, growth, well-being, problems, or destiny."[1] Here are some examples of inappropriate caretaking:

- Trying to solve people's problems for them
- Doing things for people that they are capable of and should be doing for themselves
- Trying to fix people's feelings
- Protecting people from the consequences of their choices and actions
- Trying to do people's thinking for them
- Attempting to meet people's needs without being asked to do so[2]

Underlying most such behavior is the so-called rescuer's belief that the other person is not really capable of managing on his or her own. Rescuers often learn this way of dealing with people by growing up in families in which there was substance abuse or other serious dysfunction. For such individuals, "a person with a need or problem provokes us to feel we have to do something or feel guilty,"[3] and the response to that all-too-familiar need is a desperate attempt to fix things somehow, to get things to turn out right for once. Rescuing is differentiated from true helping in that rescuing has an involuntary, compulsive quality to it, whereas true helping arises in "situations where our assistance is legitimately wanted and needed and we want to give that assistance."[4]

Unfortunately, the usual result of a rescue effort is resentment on the part of both the rescuer and the rescuee. The rescuer feels put upon about "having" to intervene, and angry that the person he or she is trying to help is not more cooperative or grateful. Meanwhile, the rescuee feels annoyed, insulted, or manipulated by the condescending interference. As Beattie put it, "People resent being told or shown they are incompetent, no matter how loudly they plead incompetency."[5] Typically, the upshot is that the rescuee somehow subverts the attempted help, and the rescuer becomes angrier than ever, and more convinced that the rescuee is incompetent.

Understanding that rescuing is a destructive, no-win proposition for both parties is the first step toward change. Even so, it can be extremely difficult for someone who has spent a lifetime trying to rescue other people to break out of that pattern. Indeed, in most settings there is not much social support for drawing a distinction between appropriate and inappropriate ways of helping, and in many people's minds rescuing "becomes inextricably entangled with being a good wife, mother, husband, brother, or Christian."[6] Women in particular tend to have been socialized to respond to what other people appear to need.

In such arrangements, then, the rescuers' compulsion to step in keeps the cycle going. And the pressure to keep responding in the same way can be external as well as internal. If rescuers try to learn how to interact more appropriately, "people may get angry at us for setting boundaries; they can't use us anymore. They may try to help us feel guilty so we will remove our boundary and return to the old system of letting them use or abuse [us]."[7] Responses to attempts to break out of the old, dysfunctional ways of doing things can take the form of expressions of anger or hurt, guilt messages, accusations, increases in problematic behavior, or even abuse.[8]

It is essential that, as spiritual directors, we learn how to offer help appropriately. Even if we do not see ourselves in the rescue scenarios described at the beginning of this chapter, we need to be attuned to whatever inclinations we might have to want to cure our directees' addictions, help them find new jobs, keep them out of debt, improve their marriages, or protect them from disappointment. Our role is not to fix difficult situations or take away discomfort but rather to accompany people as they grow through their challenges and reach out to God in them. We are doing our directees no favor by taking extensive care of them; we can, in fact, be doing them harm. A book addressed to neophyte counselors and psychotherapists pointed out that "the tendency to give advice and try to direct another's life can be especially harmful in a therapist, because it leads to excessive dependence on the part of clients and only perpetuates their tendency to look outside themselves for answers. Therapists who need to feel powerful or important may begin to think that they are indispensable to their clients or, worse still, *make* themselves so."[9]

Even before saying a word to his directee about it, Dennis has a rescue mission in mind. Rather than expressing concern to Craig about evidence of his drinking and inviting discussion about what he thinks it might mean in relationship to his Higher Power or what he thinks he might do about it, Dennis has devised a plan to confront Craig and then, presumably, talk him into accepting in-house monitoring of his alcohol intake. He seems to have lost track of the likelihood that Craig knows perfectly well where to find the nearest AA meeting, how to contact his sponsor, and what other recovery resources are available to him. And Dennis may not even realize how his own personal history could be contributing to his responses. Wouldn't it be interesting if *Craig* were to confront *Dennis* concerning his evident need to attend to his unresolved feelings about his alcoholic mother and refer him to an Al-Anon meeting?

HEROIC HELPLESSNESS

Inevitably, there are times when things go badly, when suffering persists, or when the best of everyone's efforts do not result in hoped-for change. Such times are difficult and often painful for those in helping relationships. The psychologist Margo Rivera, for example, admitted that "I much prefer dealing with my own problems [over which I usually have some degree of control] to recognizing the reality that I may not have the power to help people make the kind of changes in their lives that I would like to see and that they say they wish desperately to make."[10]

One counseling professor related how he frantically trotted out an armamentarium of therapeutic approaches in the face of his frustration and guilt over a client whose dreary life circumstances and intractable depression he and others had tried unsuccessfully to alleviate:

> I had tried to take away her emotional pain by applying techniques from all those theories I had learned in graduate school. *I was also afraid of acknowledging the depth of her*

pain. I was using theoretical interventions to avoid opening a door where I could have entered the darkness of her inner world and experienced it with her. By *overrelying on the magic of techniques to protect myself,* I had failed to hear what Sheila so desperately needed from me. . . . Everyone had wanted her to feel better, and their efforts had only made her feel guilty that she was disappointing them when their suggestions didn't work."[11] (emphasis added)

The more he tried to "fix" the client, the more she resisted his efforts. Only when he revealed to her his own feelings of helplessness over her situation and acknowledged the validity and painfulness of her feelings was there a break in the impasse in their counseling relationship.

Sometimes responses to such situations can take the form of impatience or even anger, as a way of warding off the frightening feeling of powerlessness and lack of control. For instance, someone like Esther may be regarded by her frustrated helpers as "a chronic complainer," one with whom they wish to interact as briefly and infrequently as possible. Medical personnel, whose task it is to cure illnesses, can sometimes find it especially difficult to spend time in the presence of what may seem to them to be manifest evidence of "failure."

What, then, can we as spiritual directors do in the face of pain or discouragement or defeat that just won't go away? We can be present, and we can listen. We can sit beside our directees in their darkness and validate their experiences. Margaret Guenther noted that "as hearers of stories, we can be agents of healing. . . . There is great relief in hearing that loving, trusted other acknowledge the reality of pain."[12]

And we can join them in calling upon the presence of God. Citing a crucial point made in a work by Belden Lane, the Mennonite pastor Arthur Paul Boers declared that "God meets us, works with us, comforts us, and helps us to grow in places we least expect—places of pain, brokenness, disappointment, frustration, and disillusion."[13] We can help our directees pray for healing, and help them recognize how healing can take place even in the absence of a "cure."

It takes courage to accompany people into that lonely space where things cannot be fixed. What will they want from us? How long will we have to stay? How painful will it be to hear what they tell us? Is it contagious? What if we realize that the same things could happen to us? Might it be more than we can bear?

Bill Wallace, a priest with expertise in pastoral care of the dying and bereaved, regards the choice to be present in this way as heroic: "Heroic helplessness is when the caregiver faces the limitations of her ability to make well. . . . She comes to terms with the fact that her helplessness, finally, is the most she has to offer, the precious source of empathic connection that fades unhealthy distinctions between healer and healed."[14] Ultimately, our function as spiritual directors is not to help people solve problems but rather to listen *to them* and *with them.* "The pastoral and psychotherapeutic challenge is not to fall into the sleep of anxious activity out of fear of powerlessness, but to watch and wait with those who invite us to be present with them in their forests of despair, and to accompany them through forbidden forests in which they do not want to travel alone."[15]

Notes

1. Melody Beattie, *Codependent No More: How to Stop Controlling Others and Start Caring for Yourself* (New York: Harper/Hazelden, 1987), 78.

2. Ibid., 78, 79.

3. Ibid., 83.

4. Ibid., 79.

5. Ibid., 80.

6. Ibid., 22; similarly, Anne Wilson Schaef, *Co-Dependence: Misunderstood, Mistreated* (Minneapolis: Winston Press, 1986), chapter 5.

7. Beattie, *Codependent No More*, 201.

8. Henry Cloud and John Townsend, *Boundaries: When to Say Yes, When to Say No to Take Control of Your Life* (Grand Rapids, MI: Zondervan, 1992), 240–250.

9. Gerald Corey, Marianne Schneider Corey, and Patrick Callanan, *Issues and Ethics in the Helping Professions*, 4th ed. (Pacific Grove, CA: Brooks/Cole Publishing Company, 1993), 31.

10. Margo Rivera, "I–Thou: Interpersonal Boundaries in the Therapy Relationship," in *Boundary Wars: Intimacy and Distance in Healing Relationships*, ed. Katherine Hancock Ragsdale (Cleveland: Pilgrim Press, 1996), *186*.

11. David S. Shepard, "Finding Your Way: Sometimes Life Sucks," *Counseling Today* (November 2001), 30.

12. Margaret Guenther, *Toward Holy Ground: Spiritual Directions for the Second Half of Life* (Cambridge, MA: Cowley Publications), 85.

13. Arthur Paul Boers, *Never Call Them Jerks: Healthy Responses to Difficult Behavior* (Bethesda, MD: Alban Institute, 1999), 108.

14. Bill Wallace, "Care of the Dying: Power Between, Power Under, and Powerlessness With as Means for Valuing and Balancing Boundaries and Mutuality," in *Boundary Wars,* 220.

15. Ibid., 221.

~

CHAPTER SEVEN

Referral

GAIL AND HOWARD: *Gail is an aspirant for ordination to the priesthood and works part-time in a parish as director of spiritual formation. She has developed a program of individual and group spiritual direction that has become well known throughout the community. One day Howard, a young man who is not a member of the congregation, approaches her to inquire about spiritual direction. In their initial conversation she asks him about his interest in and expectations of spiritual direction. He responds with a wide-ranging account of how distressed he has been over several failed relationships and how much he needs "radical change." When she asks him about prayer and the role of God in his life, he focuses on her questions for only a minute or two before going on in considerable detail about how various people were to blame for his unsuccessful relationships.*

BROTHER IAN AND JESSICA: *Brother Ian has had several meetings with Jessica, his newest directee. In each conversation he had the feeling that there was something important that she was not telling him, but her responses to his gentle, indirect questions had shed no light on what it might be. When she arrives for today's appointment, he notices that she looks a bit shaken and has not succeeded in covering up a large bruise on the side of her face. He greets her and, as she walks gingerly toward her chair, asks if she is all right. She pauses, looks away, sits down, and then replies quietly that she is not. It turns out that her husband has been unable to find a job since he was laid off six months ago, and several times lately he has lost control and hit her when he got angry.*

KATHLEEN AND LATASHA: *Kathleen has been coming to meet with Latasha, a spiritual director who is also a clinical social worker, for more than two years. She feels comfortable talking and praying with her director, and she has even begun to think about some areas of her life and her family history that she never paid much attention to before. Recently, though, she has started having spells of anxiety that at times get in the way of her daily activities. Tonight, having somehow survived the feeling that she was about to suffocate or faint in the subway on the way home from work, Kathleen knows she needs to talk to somebody right away. She dials Latasha's home number.*

MALCOLM AND NINA: *Malcolm and Nina have been friends ever since they went through a spiritual direction training program together several years ago. Last year Nina lost her twelve-year-old son, who was hit by a car while doing stunts on his bicycle. After the funeral she immediately resumed offering direction and working at her job as an architect, saying that what she needed most was to keep busy and get on with her life.*

Lately, Malcolm has been worried that Nina seems unusually protective of one of her directees. Without revealing the person's identity, she told him that she has a directee with whom she meets four or five times a month ("because she needs it"). She also mentioned that she takes phone calls from her at all hours and lent her money to get an apartment after a marital breakup. Malcolm is concerned that Nina's behavior toward this directee seems inappropriate for spiritual direction, and he does not think she has yet dealt forthrightly with her feelings about her son's death.

~

As spiritual directors, we need to know the limits of our competence and know what to do when directees need types of assistance other than those we are prepared to offer them. The need to consider referral arises most often at the outset of a relationship, when director and directee are in the process of discerning whether they will work together, and in an established relationship when a directee starts to experience unusual difficulties. Occasionally, even our colleagues may need assistance in recognizing the need for help for themselves.

AT THE OUTSET

In considering whether to work with someone who approaches me to ask about spiritual direction, I find it helpful to pay attention to the degree to which the potential directee can focus on the usual subject matter of spiritual direction during an hour's conversation. That is, if he or she seems to have difficulty giving thoughtful attention to questions about prayer and relationship with God and instead repeatedly expresses distress over a life crisis (as Howard does), it is likely that that person would benefit more from psychotherapy than from spiritual direction, at least at that point. The same is usually true for those in the throes of active addiction, whose needs might be better addressed first by a twelve-step program or other rehabilitation resource.

If a new directee seems reluctant or unable to adhere to the customary one-meeting-per-month schedule of spiritual direction and instead repeatedly requests additional meetings or other contact between meetings, referral also should be on the agenda. As one spiritual director put it, "A rule of thumb is that if directees need to see us more frequently [than once a month], they are likely to be in need of therapy instead."[1] However, I might invite such a person to contact me again to discuss the possibility of direction once he or she has been engaged in therapy or some other appropriate program of intervention for a while and some changes are evident.

Learning that a directee is involved in any situation of potential danger to life or health (e.g., suicide or homicide threats, domestic violence, ongoing substance abuse, harassment) should also serve as an indication that outside intervention is needed. According to *A Code of Ethics for Spiritual Directors*, "Non-licensed counselors (including spiritual directors) are not mandated by law to report cases of potential suicide, but surely have a moral duty to refer suicidal persons to mental health professionals and to be sure that referrals are acted upon." Furthermore, in instances "where there is a clear danger to another's safety or life," spiritual directors "have a duty to warn the endangered parties or their legal guardians, and are morally responsible to intervene by reporting such danger to the proper authorities."

Brother Ian will now have to discuss several questions with Jessica in response to her report of domestic violence. Are her injuries serious enough to require medical treatment? Does she think she might be in further danger if she returns home? Should she get an order of protection? What resources (e.g., relatives, emergency housing, community programs) might she draw upon at this point? How can he, as a spiritual director, appropriately support her efforts to deal with this situation? If she denies that this is a significant problem, or tells him that her husband's hitting her was somehow her fault, how can he help her consider the possibility that God might see things differently?

A third type of situation in which early referral is indicated is, of course, if a directee and I determine that we are not a good enough match. We might discern that the individual would be likely to work better in group spiritual direction, or with a male director, or a director with more background in theology, or one who takes a more literal approach to Scripture or is a member of a religious order—or simply a director with a different time schedule. In such an instance, I do my best to make sure that the potential directee does not go away feeling that she or he has somehow "failed" in spiritual direction, and I try to help with the search for another director.

WORK IN PROGRESS

Occasionally a directee who has been doing fine for some time encounters a crisis or disruptive life event. If we have already been working with this individual for a while, it may be more difficult to recognize a need for referral than it would be with a new directee. We feel comfortable with that person; he or she feels comfortable with us; nothing much has ever gone wrong with this directee before; we think we ought to be able to work through it together; we wonder whether more prayer might help, or maybe some relaxation exercises? For a spiritual director like Latasha, who happens also to be a clinical social worker, it might be especially easy to move unintentionally into a quasi-therapeutic role.

But spiritual direction is not an appropriate substitute for psychotherapy, or pastoral counseling, or medication, or a recovery program! Barring an outright miracle, spending one hour a month talking with us about God and prayer is not going to make much of a dent in someone's acute grief, eating disorder, gambling addiction, or clinical depression.

One way to help people determine if they need additional assistance is to consider whether and how the problem is disrupting their normal life. For example, has the directee recently and consistently (for two or more consecutive weeks) experienced significant impairments or changes in his or her ability to

* eat;
* sleep;
* work;
* study;
* relax;

- get around;
- make decisions;
- fulfill family responsibilities;
- fulfill financial responsibilities;
- carry on a reasonably focused conversation;
- participate in social activities?

Significant, ongoing alterations in any of these abilities suggest the possibility of a problem in need of attention; the more areas of functioning that are affected, the more likely it is that referral for further help is warranted.

Sometimes spiritual directors are called upon to assist directees who are going through what seems to be a period of spiritual darkness, or "dark night of the soul." Such experiences may be characterized by a feeling of dryness and emptiness in prayer and a profoundly disheartening sense of the absence of God. This sort of "dark night" has been written about for centuries by mystics such as John of the Cross and regarded as a classic phenomenon of spiritual development. Unfortunately, it is not easy for most of us to distinguish among "psychological reactions to spiritual experiences, spiritual experiences that are mistaken for primary psychological changes, psychological phenomena that masquerade as spiritual experiences, and a host of other combinations."[2] Some sources of assistance in understanding such experiences and discerning which can be worked with appropriately through spiritual direction and which might best be addressed by psychotherapeutic intervention are Gerald G. May's *Care of Mind, Care of Spirit: A Psychiatrist Explores Spiritual Direction*; Mary Ann Woodman's article titled "Dark Nights" in the journal *Presence*; and *Spiritual Emergency: When Personal Transformation Becomes a Crisis*, edited by Stanislav Grof and Christina Grof. I, for one, find the challenge of making such distinctions so daunting that my rule of thumb is "Whenever in doubt, consult a therapist and consider referral."

When preparing to make a referral for therapy, it is important for a director to do some personal discernment as well. I ask myself whether there is any chance that my motivation in making the referral is primarily to avoid dealing with some troublesome issue of my own. Or do I wish to avoid further contact with a person whose opinions or demands or lack of "progress" are making me uncomfortable?[3] If referral is indeed warranted, I need to be clear and unambivalent in my own mind about pursuing it. Otherwise, it can be all too easy to be sidetracked by assertions from the directee such as "Oh, but I couldn't possibly go to anyone else! You are the *only* one I can talk to about this!" According to *A Code of Ethics for Spiritual Directors*, "Directors should not agree to continue as the sole helping person for someone who obviously needs psychological help and refuses to seek it upon such recommendation. To do so may prevent the person in need of aid from reaching out for it 'because I have a spiritual director.'" In fact, failure to make an appropriate referral can in some instances be regarded legally as a form of negligence.[4]

The psychiatrist and spiritual director Gerald May pointed out that the referral process should not consist simply of telling a directee to go for therapy or other assistance and then providing the names of some resources. "If counseling or psychotherapy is really going to be of help, the individual must recognize the need and have some personal motivation."[5] He recommended that the referral decision be arrived at mutually and prayerfully by director and directee. "Even in situations of psychological crisis," he noted, "there is time for at least some prayerful attention and calling upon the Lord for guidance."[6]

When I begin the process of discussing with a directee the possibility of referral to another source of help, I take care to explain why I am making such a suggestion. I also like to emphasize my positive view of the step I am recommending. Telling a directee that I consider the problem "an important issue that deserves the best kind of attention we can find" is likely to be more helpful than saying, "This problem is way out of *my* range! I've got to send you to somebody *else* for that!" I also explore whether the directee may already be acquainted with some appropriate resources. Often someone will reply to my raising the question of re-ferral with "Oh, yes, actually I'd been thinking about going back to my therapist about this" or "My cousin keeps telling me about this great support group. Maybe it's time I checked it out."

In the course of making a referral for psychotherapy, I also ad-vise the directee to inform the therapist that she or he also meets with a spiritual director.[7] And I offer the option of taking some time off from spiritual direction if that seems best. One of the things I especially appreciate about spiritual direction is how many choices there are for proceeding in such situations. For instance, if Latasha and Kathleen decide to continue meeting without in-terruption while Kathleen is getting established with a therapist, they might elect to spend more of their direction meetings in struc-tured prayer activities for a while, rather than continuing to dis-cuss the family issues which might further contribute to the directee's anxiety.

IMPAIRED COLLEAGUES

Once in a while we may come across information that sug-gests another spiritual director might be behaving inappropriately toward a directee. Neither the Spiritual Directors International *Guidelines for Ethical Conduct* nor the Center for Sacred Psy-chology's *Code of Ethics for Spiritual Directors* addresses this issue, but ethics codes for several mental health professions have done so. According to the American Counseling Association's *Code of Ethics and Standards of Practice*, "When counselors have reasonable cause to believe that another counselor is violating an ethical standard, they attempt first to resolve the issue informally with the other counselor if feasible, providing that such action does not violate confidentiality rights that might be involved."[8] Likewise, the *Ethical Principles of Psychologists and Code of Con-duct* specifies that "when psychologists believe that there may have been an ethical violation by another psychologist, they at-tempt to resolve the issue by bringing it to the attention of that individual if an informal resolution appears appropriate and the intervention does not violate any confidentiality rights that may be involved."[9] The American Psychoanalytic Association's *Principles and Standards of Ethics for Psychoanalysts* further specifies that "the psychoanalyst should strive to protect the patients of colleagues . . . observed to be deficient in competence or known to be engaged in behavior with the potential of affecting such patients adversely. S/he should urge such colleagues to seek help. Information about unethical or impaired conduct by any member of the profession should be reported to the appropriate committee at local or national levels."[10]

Spiritual directors do not have local or national ethics committees, and sometimes—for good reason—we might be inclined to comment along the lines of "But who's to say it's not inspired by the Holy Spirit?" about practices that differ from the usual. Although Nina's reported behavior toward her directee may not explicitly violate the letter of either of the published codes of ethics for spiritual directors, it does seem that there could be a problem. Spiritual direction does not customarily involve frequent meetings or midnight telephone conversations or the lending of money, and Malcolm may well be correct in his suspicion that Nina's unacknowledged and unprocessed grief may be affecting her work with her directee. Perhaps the most appropriate response would be for him to express his concerns to her unequivocally and compassionately, and to offer to help her find some sources of assistance. Had this been a situation that more explicitly involved unethical behavior harmful to a directee, and had the director denied the need for help, an appropriate response might have been to consult with other spiritual directors to discern what to do next.

REFERRAL TOOL KIT

Ideally, a spiritual director should compile and regularly update a list of referral and consultation resources available in the community, such as the following:

- Several other spiritual directors
- Several therapists, preferably including pastoral counselors, marriage and family counselors, and psychiatrists who prescribe medication
- Low-cost clinics
- Twelve-step groups (such as Alcoholics Anonymous, Al-Anon, Overeaters Anonymous) and other addiction recovery resources
- Other types of support groups
- Crisis centers and hotlines

For an excellent and more extensive discussion of issues surrounding the need for and process of referral, see Gerald May's *Care of Mind, Care of Spirit*, particularly chapter 7 ("Disorder: Psychiatric Syndromes") and chapter 8 ("Colleagueship: Referral, Consultation, and Collaboration").

Notes

1. Jonathan Foster, "Liability Issues in a Ministry of Spiritual Direction," *Presence* 2:3 (September 1996), 52.

2. Gerald G. May, *Care of Mind, Care of Spirit: A Psychiatrist Explores Spiritual Direction* (HarperSanFrancisco, 1992), 102.

3. For more about this self-examination process, see May, *Care of Mind, Care of Spirit*, 179–183.

4. Sally A. Johnson, "Legal Issues in Clergy Sexual Boundary Violation Matters," in *Boundary Wars: Intimacy and Distance in Healing Relationships*, ed. Katherine Hancock Ragsdale (Cleveland: Pilgrim Press, 1996), 153.

5. May, *Care of Mind, Care of Spirit*, 182.

6. Ibid., 183.

7. Spiritual Directors International's *Guidelines for Ethical Conduct* recommends that a directee "inform his or her therapist about being in spiritual direction." Hedberg, Caprio et al.'s *A Code of Ethics for Spiritual Directors* further suggests that, as an ethical courtesy as well as a legal protection, "the directee should be asked to clear the spiritual direction arrangement with [the therapist], and to get a written acknowledgment of the addition of spiritual direction to the . . . treatment plan." For a contrasting view of the latter suggestion, see Gerald G. May, "Professional-

izing Spiritual Direction," *Shalem News On Line* 24:3 (Fall 2000), http://www.shalem.org/sn/24.3gm.html.

8. American Counseling Association, *ACA Code of Ethics and Standards of Practice*, http://www.counseling.org/site/PageServer?pagename=resources_ethics#ce, Title H.2.d.

9. American Psychological Association, *Ethical Principles of Psychologists and Code of Conduct* (Washington, DC: American Psychological Association, 1992), Title 8.04.

10. American Psychoanalytic Association, *Principles and Standards of Ethics for Psychoanalysts*, http://www.apsa.org/ethics901.htm, Title VIII.

≈

CHAPTER EIGHT

Self-Care

SISTER OLIVIA AND SISTER PERPETUA: *Sister Olivia has been a spiritual director for many years. Lately the demand for spiritual direction has increased while the number of sisters in her community available to respond to this need has decreased. To make matters worse, a few months ago a member of the community, Sister Perpetua, suffered a stroke and does not seem likely to recover enough to resume offering spiritual direction. So Sister Olivia and the other four sisters in the convent have divided up Sister Perpetua's responsibilities, including meeting with her many directees and conducting the retreats she had scheduled. This means that Sister Olivia has added six new, grieving directees to the barely manageable number she had already, along with additional retreats and household tasks. Several times lately she has caught herself dreading the prospect of yet another direction meeting, or feeling too impatient or irritated to listen well to a directee. Last night, while helping Sister Perpetua into her wheelchair, she had a dizzy spell that made her wonder whether she might be about to have a stroke herself.*

QUENTIN AND REBECCA: *Recently ordained, Quentin is a curate in a large parish. He finds the work exciting and rewarding, but lately he is beginning to have difficulty getting around to all the tasks the rector has delegated to him. One of the many responsibilities he enthusiastically accepted is offering spiritual direction to people from neighboring congregations. His first directee, Rebecca, is now in a spiritual direction program and has begun seeing directees herself. When Quentin arrives at his office today, breathless and twenty minutes late for his meeting with Rebecca, he begins to describe to her, by way of apology, how hectic his life has been lately. She listens so patiently and seems to understand so well that the hour is almost over before he realizes they are still talking about his problems.*

SOFIA AND THOMAS: *Sofia is a spiritual director who also manages her family's small insurance brokerage. Her mother died two years ago, and now she is helping her father arrange for hospice care since his latest round of chemotherapy treatments failed to slow the progress of his cancer. Her directee, Thomas, recently lost his partner to AIDS, and today he and Sofia are talking about where God might be for him in his bereavement. At one point they pause to pray together for Thomas's partner, and during the prayer Sofia begins to sob audibly. After they have finished praying, her directee asks why she seems so upset. Attempting to reply, she finds she cannot even distinguish between her responses to the grief he has been expressing and her feelings about her own past and potential losses.*

~

We may be called by God to offer spiritual direction, but it is always helpful to remember that we are *not* God! Much as we might like to be able to do everything we want, need, or are asked to do, we simply can't. In a society where people are now expected to be speedy, efficient multitasking experts, it is a challenge to recall that the ministry of spiritual direction demands precisely the opposite sort of orientation—slowing down, focusing, and silence—in order to listen for God. To say no to a request to take care of something, to turn down a legitimate call for help from someone in need, or to admit to ourselves and to others that we cannot do everything can be extremely difficult as well as radically countercultural. We need to bear in mind that "people are not going to feel heard by someone who is in a hurry, nor will they feel that they can approach someone who always seems to have too much going on in their lives [sic]. . . . Those who favor a rhythm of pausing to pay attention to the ordinary, vernacular life will be more able themselves to value, accept, and confirm the pace and nature of the journey of another's soul."[1]

KNOW YOUR LIMITS

In a section titled "Directors Guard Their Health," *A Code of Ethics for Spiritual Directors* states that among "the causes of stress and burnout in ministry [are] . . . over-scheduling, too many directees, and too little prayer and reflection time before and after sessions." And the Spiritual Directors International *Guidelines for Ethical Conduct* recommends that "spiritual directors meet their needs outside the direction relationship in a variety of ways, especially by . . . self-care, wisely balancing time for worship, work, leisure, family, and personal relationships," and that "spiritual directors recognize the limits of energy by restricting the number of directees."

One signal that we are trying to do too much is if we experience symptoms of stress. These can be physical (e.g., hypertension, headaches) as well as mental (e.g., irritability, difficulty concentrating). For Sister Olivia, the factors triggering her stress might be a combination of having too many responsibilities, having to do too much of the same activity (spiritual direction) for too long a period, and her emotional response to being reminded of the daunting challenges of aging. If her life continues this way, she might indeed develop a physical illness. At the very least, the fact that she is beginning to dread meeting with directees indicates that she needs to take a break from offering spiritual direction. And her religious community must begin discerning how they might deal with the changed circumstances in their household without subjecting all of them to unmanageable stress. Perhaps, for example, they could identify other spiritual direction resources in their area that they can call upon for assistance with their current overload of directees and retreats or look for volunteers in their neighborhood to help with household tasks.

A second indication that we may be working beyond our personal limits is if, like Quentin, we are having difficulty meeting our commitments to directees. More than occasional instances of lateness, missed appointments, or forgetting to do what we told someone we would do (e.g., bring a particular book or look something up) may mean that we are trying to juggle more responsibilities than we can reliably handle. Like many starting out in a new line of work, Quentin is admirably energetic and eager to try his hand at many projects. But such enthusiasm can give way to disillusionment or even burnout if he finds, over and over again, that he cannot keep up and experiences failure as a consequence. He might also become discouraged when he discovers that people are not always appreciative of his extraordinary efforts, that his self-expectations are unrealistically high, or that, human nature being what it is, even the best of his efforts seem to produce little visible change. Quentin might be well advised to seek guidance in prioritizing and determining how many things he can reasonably expect to achieve given the time he has available. If he is going to continue offering spiritual direction, joining a peer supervision group would be recommended as well.

A third sign that some self-examination is called for is if we are having trouble keeping our personal needs well to the background while meeting with directees. Linda Julian noted that "directors who talk about themselves, share their own experiences at any length, air their own ideas and opinions, give lots of helpful advice, let you tempt them into intellectual discussions are indulging themselves and failing in the quite difficult practice of getting themselves out of the way in the spiritual direction exchange."[2] Because sharing our own experiences can be an appropriate tool in spiritual direction, it is not always so easy to figure out when our self-revelation has shaded over into self-indulgence, especially if our directees are too polite to call it to our attention or seem eager to hear us talk about ourselves. But sometimes it is obvious: for instance, there is no question that Quentin ought to be discussing his work pressures with his rector, not his directee.

A fourth indicator that more attention to self-care may be needed is if we react overly strongly to what a directee is telling us. Just as directees are subject to transference reactions, we are subject to countertransference (emotional responses to directees that in fact arise from our own issues). If something a directee says makes us feel extremely angry, sad, anxious, enamored, or energized, or if we find ourselves dwelling on the conversation for days afterward, we ought to pay attention to what those reactions might be telling us about ourselves.

When we are going through a period of great disruption in our own lives, it is essential that we discern whether we are still fit to offer spiritual direction. Although some degree of projective identification[3] with a directee's emotions may be appropriate on occasion, it seems more likely that Sofia is so overwhelmed by her own feelings that she is not relating reliably to Thomas's feelings *as his*. She may be under so much pressure, with a gravely ill parent and a family business to run, that it would be wise for her to seek support for herself in grief counseling or a bereavement group. It is also possible that her directee's issues and her own are so similar that she is not capable of looking at them from a sufficiently objective distance at this point. If she were to continue to overidentify with directees or have trouble keeping her own difficulties out of the foreground during meetings with them, she would be well advised to take a sabbatical from offering spiritual direction until her emotional responses take up less space. The example of Malcolm and Nina in chapter 7 is also relevant to this discussion.

In all these instances of overcommitment, it is important to note that the process of addressing the problem need not be, and indeed should not be, an isolated one. Sister Olivia should work with her community toward improving their arrangements to meet their responsibilities. Quentin should consult with more experienced peers and colleagues to determine how better to handle his work pressures. Sofia needs the support of others in getting through her personal crisis and deciding whether she should take time off from offering direction. And all of them need the support of God. As they discern how to proceed, prayer should be central.

THE INDISPENSABILITY TRAP

Perhaps one of the reasons we find it difficult to take time off or say no when asked to do something is that we tend to think we are indispensable. What will happen, we may wonder, if we are not available all the time to manage things in our competent, inimitable way? What will become of the people who depend on us? Or (if we can admit to this particular concern), what will become of *us* if we or others should discover that we are not so indispensable after all?

One of the most enlightening experiences of my career occurred about twenty-five years ago, when I had to take a leave from my job as a college counselor in order to complete my graduate studies. My responsibilities included teaching, directing a major college program, and counseling a large caseload of students. I was worried about how the students and colleagues who relied on me every day would manage in my absence, but I also knew I had to finish the degree in order to keep the job in the long run. So a faculty member from another department who had counseling and administrative credentials—and a personal style quite different from mine—was assigned to take over my tasks, and off, with great misgivings, I went.

When I returned a year later, I discovered that all traces of my presence at the college, including my files, were gone. Many of the people I recognized in the hallway seemed surprised to hear I'd been away, and there were some who did not even appear to know who I was. Once I recovered from the shock of feeling so easily replaced and forgotten, though, I began to notice that things were going along just fine. Students had been helped by the person who took over my responsibilities. My former program was running at least as smoothly as when I'd been in charge of it. And then I began to feel a profound sense of freedom. I was capable and valuable, but evidently I was *not* essential after all. I could take time off if I needed to, and someone else would manage. Even if the job wasn't done the way I would do it, it would still get done. I soon reintegrated myself into the life of the college and offered my own gifts in my own style again. But the burden of thinking that I was irreplaceable in that job would never have the same weight.

Even so, I have to admit that my old way of thinking reasserts itself from time to time. Not long ago I found myself momentarily frantic when, too ill with flu to leave the house, I had to cancel appointments with several directees on short notice. As it developed, of course, the directees were neither devastated by the loss of an opportunity to meet with me that day nor impaired in their spiritual progress by the lack of my input. There are indeed a few situations in life where we are not so readily dispensable (breast-feeding a newborn comes to mind), but spiritual direction is not—and certainly shouldn't be—among them. We can be important without being indispensable.

"What is this that you are doing for the people? Why do you sit alone, while all the people stand around you from morning until evening?" inquired Jethro in Exodus 18:13–27 as he saw his son-in-law Moses struggling to handle overwhelming responsibilities by himself. "What you are doing is not good. You will surely wear yourself out, both you and these people with you. For the task is too heavy for you; you cannot do it alone." Jethro made the essential point that Moses's single-handed approach was likely to have detrimental effects not just on him but also on the people he was trying to help. He persuaded Moses to go recruit some trustworthy others to assist him with his work, whereupon everyone had an easier time of it and the entire community benefited.

Another of my favorite readings on the topic of indispensability and burnout comes from an anonymous *Forward Day by Day* author who commented on a theme from Psalm 69 ("Zeal for your house has eaten me up"):

> No matter how important the job, it is nothing in comparison with you, who are infinitely precious in God's sight. If the task at hand is drawing you away from the daily knowledge of God's love, then someone else needs to carry the burden for a time: you cannot work for the greater glory of the Kingdom if you starve your own soul.
>
> Remember that God can achieve whatever is at hand with or without you; the task was put in front of you in order to draw you into the mind of Christ. Whether you complete the task or not is supremely unimportant; whether it brings you closer to God is all that matters. Your achievements, as wonderful as they may be, are not the basis for God's heartbreaking love for you.[4]

REMEMBER THE SABBATH

An excellent way to address our tendencies to overwork and to overestimate our irreplaceability is to incorporate some sabbath observance into our lives. Sabbath time requires us to stop doing what we usually do and surrender for a while our efforts to act upon and change the world. If we regularly suspend our usual activities and simply let things be, it is likely to become apparent to us, over time, that our intervention is not continually required. In discussing sabbath practices drawn from a wide range of spiritual traditions, the minister and therapist Wayne Muller noted, "The problem is not necessarily working hard, the problem is working so hard and long without rest that we begin to imagine that we're the ones making everything happen. We begin to feel a growing, gnawing sense of responsibility and grandiosity about how important our work is and how we can't stop because everything is on our shoulders. We forget that forces much larger than we are, in fact, do most of the work."[5]

Muller, in his book *Sabbath*, emphasized that sabbath observance ought to be about relaxation and enjoyment, not prohibitions and deprivation. If we take time out to lie fallow, stop working on problems, give thanks for what we already have instead of striving after what we do not have, and allow ourselves to have some fun, we will be better equipped to listen for God. As Muller put it, "There comes a moment in our striving when more effort actually becomes counterproductive, when our frantic busyness only muddies the waters of our wisdom and understanding. When we become still and allow our life to rest, we feel a renewal of energy and gradual clarity of perception."[6] We would do well to remember how often Jesus regularly (and sometimes abruptly) withdrew from the demands of his ministry to spend time in prayer alone or with his disciples.

How often have we advised our directees to include some sort of sabbath time in their lives? How well do we follow our own advice? If we are not setting a good example for them at present, what can we do about that?

RESPECT YOUR NEEDS

It is *not* selfish to acknowledge and attend to our needs for rest, companionship, solitude, recreation, counsel, encouragement, and people to whom we can safely tell the unvarnished truth. Speaking for myself, I would not even attempt to offer spiritual direction unless I had a spiritual director and a peer supervision group to support me, keep me honest, and help me grow; friends and family to work and play with me; and access to a therapist to help me understand countertransference issues that crop up. Without such resources, there would be a greater likelihood that I might start to rely, inappropriately, on my directees to meet some of those needs.

Sandra Lommasson Pickens pointed out, "The relationship

between director and directee [should] not be used as a place of personal support of [*sic*] social/play activity by the director. Basic self care is key here so that the director assumes responsibility for maintaining his or her own physical, emotional, and spiritual well-being. This includes a balance of work and leisure, commitment to one's own spiritual direction process, and the cultivation of supportive personal relationships."[7]

According to *A Code of Ethics for Spiritual Directors*, "Wise directors know that stress in themselves is detrimental to those coming for assistance and that a large part of being a 'playable instrument for God' depends upon their own fitness." The authors of this code listed some causes of stress as "over-scheduling, too many directees, and too little prayer and reflection time before and after sessions." To that list I would add family or personal difficulties and work conflicts.

In order for us to be "playable instruments for God," we have to care effectively for ourselves and to recognize the importance of maintaining a healthy balance between connection and separateness. As Caroline Westerhoff put it, "Boundaries separate and define us so that we can be together. If we do not assert who we are and what we are about—if we try to be everything to everybody—we finally will have nothing to offer anyone."[8]

Notes

1. Jean Stairs, *Listening for the Soul: Pastoral Care and Spiritual Direction* (Minneapolis: Fortress Press, 2000), 20.

2. Linda Julian, "On Finding a Spiritual Director," *Quarterly Newsletter of the Order of St. Helena* 20:1 (March 1999), http://www.osh.org/ministries/Ministries(LJarticle).html.

3. The psychologist Margo Rivera described projective identification as "the dropping of the barrier between two individuals such that, as therapist, I sometimes feel my client's feelings transiently as if they were my own and thus am able to understand what my client is feeling" ("I–Thou: Interpersonal Boundaries in the Therapy Relationship," in *Boundary Wars: Intimacy and Distance in Healing Relationships*, ed. Katherine Hancock Ragsdale [Cleveland: Pilgrim Press, 1996], 180).

4. *Forward Day by Day*, 65:1 (February–April 1999), 34.

5. Wayne Muller, in Mary Nurrie Stearns, "A Time of Sacred Rest: An Interview with Wayne Muller," *Personal Transformation*, http://www.personaltransformation.com/Muller.html, accessed November 1, 2002.

6. Wayne Muller, *Sabbath: Restoring the Sacred Rhythm of Rest* (New York: Bantam Books, 1999), 26.

7. Sandra Lommasson Pickens, "Looking at Dual/Multiple Relationships: Danger or Opportunity?" *Presence* 2:2 (May 1996), 57.

8. Caroline Westerhoff, *Good Fences: The Boundaries of Hospitality* (Cambridge, MA: Cowley Publications, 1999), 53.

~

CHAPTER NINE

For Directees: What to Expect

URSULA AND VIRGINIA: *Ursula has been interested in receiving spiritual direction ever since she participated in an Elderhostel program at a monastery. She once heard someone mention that her pastor, Virginia, is an experienced director, and she thinks she would feel comfortable talking with her about her spiritual questions and concerns. But when Ursula asks Virginia to be her spiritual director, Virginia explains that she does not direct people from her own congregation and refers her instead to a spirituality center in a neighboring suburb.*

WANDA AND XAVIER: *Wanda was raised in a home where God was depicted as a demanding, punitive taskmaster. She grew up believing that life was a minefield of temptations to sin and that God was continually disappointed in her for failing to measure up to "His" high standards. Now that she is in her thirties and has two young children of her own, she wants to explore other ways of thinking about God.*

Recently she started meeting with Xavier, a spiritual director at a church that is very different from the one in which she was raised. During their first conversation, when she tried to describe how God had seemed when she was growing up,

Xavier began telling her that God was actually all-forgiving, all-accepting, and all-loving. At first she was delighted and relieved to encounter such radically different God-imagery. But now that they are meeting for the fourth time, she realizes she is starting to feel impatient whenever her spiritual director interrupts her musings to tell her what God is "really" like. She wonders how he can be so certain about the nature of God. She also wonders if he would be offended if she told him that his certainty is beginning to remind her a lot of her parents.

YELENA AND ZACH: *Yelena has been coming to Zach for spiritual direction for almost a year. She undertook direction with the expectation that her director would prescribe a regimen of meditation, fasting, retreats, and pilgrimages that would enable her to attain more exalted spiritual states. But Zach has proven to be a disappointment in that regard. All he does, month after month, is suggest that she participate in church services faithfully, do some Bible reading, sit in silence for twenty minutes twice a day, say Compline at night, or journal about the spiritual implications of the work she does. She thinks such mundane approaches are dull and not very relevant to her needs, and she wonders if it is time to look for a spiritual director who has a better understanding of the holy.*

ANGELO AND BARBARA: *Angelo has been active in his church for several years, and lately he has started to wonder whether he might be called to ordained ministry. At first he thought this feeling was only a passing fancy and did not want to say anything about it to anyone. But recently he began discussing it with his spiritual director, Barbara, a priest from a nearby parish. One day at a diocesan committee meeting an acquaintance comes up to him and says, "Hey, Angelo, I hear you're thinking about becoming a priest! I think that's great. Have you met with the discernment committee yet?" He is taken aback, especially when he realizes that the source of the infor-*

mation must have been Barbara, the only person to whom he has confided his tentative sense of vocation.

~

Often it seems to me that spiritual direction is one of the best kept secrets in the Church today. I myself had never even heard the term until I happened upon a book called *Holy Listening: The Art of Spiritual Direction* in a cathedral gift shop one hot summer afternoon shortly after it was published. I was attracted first by the strikingly beautiful illustration on the cover, and then by the words "holy" and "spiritual." Leafing through the book, I discovered that it was about how to *be* a spiritual director—which meant, I imagined, that it was written for people who were vastly more religious than I was. Still, somehow I couldn't bring myself to leave the shop without buying it. At that point my opinion of my spiritual state made me worry that the person at the cash register might exclaim, "Wait a minute—this book is not for you! You're a spiritual *disaster*, not a spiritual director!"

From reading *Holy Listening* I learned a lot about what spiritual direction might be like, and I emerged from the book eager to talk with a spiritual director. Even so, it took me nearly a year to work up the courage to start looking for one, and then many more months to approach the person who was eventually recommended to me.

FINDING A DIRECTOR

What made me, perhaps like many others, feel so hesitant and unworthy when I first sought out spiritual direction? A relationship with a director involves great intimacy and requires great trust, with the potential for us to reveal our aspirations, misgivings, shortcomings, questionable motives, and even sins. And we are coming to talk with another person about how we relate to God. Margaret Guenther noted, "We live in a time when most of us can talk easily about sex, somewhat less comfortably about death, and only with the greatest difficulty about our relationship with God. To inquire how people pray is to ask *the* intimate question."[1] It seems as if practically everyone I have ever met feels like an outsider in some way, and many people seem to harbor some suspicion that their ideas or behavior in relation to religion must be inadequate or "wrong." Is it any wonder, then, that we might feel vulnerable when we approach spiritual direction?

It may help to keep in mind that all directors are (or should be) directees as well, and most of us remember quite well what it was like to receive spiritual direction for the first time. No doubt many of us have felt as intimidated as Hal did in the example in chapter 2. Remember also that, contrary to my initial impression, being a spiritual director is not about being "holy," or even about being wise. The controlling-sounding title "director" is often misunderstood. One author pointed out that "a correct understanding considers a director not as one who gives orders but rather as one who points directions."[2] Another noted that good spiritual directors should be neither authoritarian nor directive but rather "inconspicuous channels for the working of the Holy Spirit."[3] Another variously characterized a spiritual director as a prayer companion ("friends who help us over the rough spots"), a water boy ("gives no instruction to the players, nor [calls] the signals . . . is simply available when needed"), a matchmaker ("brings the directee and God together into a closer relationship . . . then fades into the background"), and a navigator (does not pilot the plane but advises "the pilot about visibility, wind, and weather conditions").[4] "The director must impress upon the directee that the Lord is the first and primary director. The director is only the voice crying in the wilderness preparing the way for the Lord's entrance."[5]

The process of finding a spiritual director should begin with prayer, "asking God to guide your search and to open your eyes to the possibilities available to you."[6] It also might be useful to speak with someone who is familiar with spiritual direction (e.g., parish clergy) to help you decide whether direction is the best resource for what you are seeking. Sometimes, what feels like a need for spiritual direction might be better addressed by counseling or psychotherapy (help with working through problems), confession (the Sacrament of Reconciliation), education (Bible study, reading groups, or theology courses), or spiritual friendship (mutual conversation of fellow seekers). Group spiritual direction or discernment groups offered by churches and spirituality centers are further alternatives to one-on-one direction. Discussing various forms the ministry of spiritual direction might take, Henri J. Nouwen commented, "I think that it would be a mistake to think only in terms of individual directors. There simply will not be enough people nor enough time to offer this type of ministry. It is important that we are thinking about a ministry in which we help one another to practice the disciplines of the Church . . . and thus live a life in which we become more and more sensitive to the ongoing presence of God in our lives."[7]

It can be discouraging if you encounter difficulty in finding a spiritual director, or if the director you ask does not agree to work with you. Many geographic areas seem to have few directors. Or a director may not be able to take on any additional directees at the time you inquire (as happened to me with the first director I contacted). Or director and directee may turn out not to be the right match. It is essential that both parties give serious attention to discerning whether they should work together. Writing about the implications of a director's saying no to a prospective directee, Alan Jones pointed out that "the one in search of direction should be encouraged to see [the 'no'] as a sign of the wisdom or weakness of the director (sometimes both), and be helped to find the right person. The 'no' of course can come from either party and might take half an hour or two or three sessions to emerge. It is very important for each person not to feel forced or constrained to enter prematurely or hastily into such a relationship."[8] If, for instance, like Ursula, you approach a member of the clergy at your place of worship and are told that he or she is not able to work with you, you should not take it as a personal rejection. Many priests, ministers, and rabbis have decided to rule out directing their own parishioners in order to avoid becoming involved in dual relationships (see chapter 4).

The Shalem Institute for Spiritual Formation advises seekers of spiritual direction that "it will probably take some time to find the right person for you. If God is in the felt need for a director, however, then it is safe to assume that the Spirit will eventually provide the resources you need. The key is to remain patient yet diligent in the waiting, to trust God in the process, remaining attentive to the direction of the Spirit."[9]

Is It a Good Enough Match?

Once you have located a director with whom to try out a working relationship, you are entitled to know what to expect. Many directors will enter into a formal or informal covenant with directees, covering issues such as meeting schedules, payment, contact outside of meetings, and confidentiality. For a discussion of what such a covenant might be like, see chapter 2. It is also appropriate to ask about the ethical guidelines or principles the director follows. Two sets of guidelines are included as appendixes in this book.

Discerning whether there is a good enough match between directee and director is in fact an ongoing task. Although much evaluation of goodness-of-fit takes place in the first several meetings, the process should be revisited whenever significant feelings of discomfort, dissatisfaction, or stagnation crop up. Like any other growth process, spiritual direction is not always comfortable, and so it may not be easy to distinguish between discomfort with direction and discomfort with the director. It is essential that any concerns about the relationship be talked about frankly and prayed about honestly by both director and directee, together as well as separately.

Wanda is looking for help in exploring ways of thinking about and relating to God that are different from those she learned as a child. By repeatedly interrupting her attempts to do so in order to tell her what God is "really" like, Xavier seems to be short-circuiting, rather than fostering and encouraging, her exploration. If a directee seems to be getting off track in some way, it is certainly the responsibility of the spiritual director to point that out and initiate discussion about it. But a good director should also give directees room and support to examine various points of view, to listen for God, and to find their way toward their own conclusions. Writing about hospitality in spiritual direction, Gerald M. Fagin asked spiritual directors, "Can we create a space where a person does not have to accept or conform to our ideas of God and the spiritual life, but rather can find their own unique relationship with God?"[10]

Wanda, then, should not hesitate to share with Xavier her reactions to his telling her what God is like. Spiritual direction should be a place where directees are invited to say what they truly think, and it is not supposed to be about the director's ego or self-image. If Xavier is secure enough about himself to hear Wanda's criticism without becoming defensive, he will acknowledge her feelings, resolve to move his beliefs on this topic out of the foreground, and start supporting her in her own exploration. If he seems insulted or hurt by her comments or continues to try to persuade her to adopt his views, he is probably not the right director for her.

Likewise, Yelena should feel free to speak up about her concern that Zach might not be addressing the needs and expectations which brought her to spiritual direction. It is possible that his approach is not the best match for her. In this case, however, it is at least as likely that Zach is trying to show his directee how spiritual growth and connection with God are day-by-day processes, accessible through ordinary activities. In a pamphlet on what to expect in spiritual direction, Alan Jones described the dissatisfaction some directees feel when their directors make seemingly mundane suggestions: "Often the next step is unspectacular and so modest and apparently trivial as to make one angry. 'Here I was all ready for martyrdom and you suggest that I get up a little earlier!'"[11] In such instances, Jones's recommendations have included reading 2 Kings 5:1–19, about Elisha's healing of Naaman. If indeed Zach is attempting to help Yelena learn about paths to "the holy" that do not proceed by way of spiritual highs, an honest discussion between them should at least make that clear.

In any event, it is not realistic to expect a perfect fit. Directors, like everyone else, vary greatly in their strengths, personalities, and points of view. Although a sense of familiarity and comfort may help get things started, it is not necessary for a director and directee to have a great deal in common in order to have a good working relationship. Much of my own best learning has been facilitated by interaction with people whose views and approaches were dissimilar to mine in significant ways.

WHAT ELSE SHOULD I KNOW?

The spiritual direction relationship is one in which a directee may not always feel comfortable, since encouraging growth often involves nudging people out of their accustomed ways of thinking and being. It is, however, a relationship in which a directee should always feel *safe*. If something happens that feels seriously wrong to you, respect that feeling, ask God for guidance, and speak up! Angelo's spiritual director committed a serious error by revealing information to others about him. Even if Barbara's intention had been to pave the way for his possible entry into the ordination process, I know of no code of ethics that would find this breach of confidentiality excusable. Angelo should make a point of telling her about this incident and how it affected him, and the two of them will need to work on its implications for their relationship. Directors who are not consistently able to resist the temptation to gossip, name-drop, or brag about their directees will eventually find that their directees have difficulty trusting them.

Some other examples of developments that call for consideration in the direction relationship include sexual attraction, excessive dependency, ongoing hostility, unreliability, and differences of opinion that are severe enough to impede free discussion. The preceding chapters include discussion of a wide range of issues which may arise in spiritual direction.

Finally, it should be noted that spiritual direction differs from other helping relationships in that it is not time-limited. Whereas in therapy or counseling it is usually considered time to stop when there has been significant improvement with respect to major issues (or, all too often these days, when the insurance coverage runs out), a direction relationship can continue for as long as both parties agree that is working well. According to *A Code of Ethics for Spiritual Directors*, "a helpful guideline for evaluation is whether or not the spiritual direction relationship is bearing fruit in a directee's life. . . . Another simple touchstone for evaluation is a comparison of the directee's spiritual life as it was when the relationship began with the way it is now." It is neither unusual nor inappropriate to leave spiritual direction or move on to another director when there is clear evidence that the fruitfulness of a particular arrangement is waning. When it is time for a relationship to terminate, it may help "to remind oneself over and over again that the true director is God and that relationships never stay the same. They grow and change."[12] Spiritual directors should understand this and act accordingly: "When directees terminate, directors freely and graciously release them with no attempt to dissuasion. . . . One must never cling to directees but, rather, try to find ways to ease the termination process if this is indicated by God's movement in the other's heart."[13]

WHERE TO FIND MORE INFORMATION

There are many resources available on the topic of spiritual direction, a broad range of which are included in the bibliography. Here are a few that may be of particular interest to those who wish to find out more about spiritual direction:

Books
* Tilden Edwards, *Spiritual Director, Spiritual Companion: Guide to Tending the Soul*. New York: Paulist Press, 2001.

- Margaret Guenther, *Holy Listening: The Art of Spiritual Direction.* Cambridge: Cowley Publications, 1992.
- David E. Rosage, *Beginning Spiritual Direction.* Ann Arbor, MI: Servant Publications, 1994.

Pamphlets

- Alan Jones, *What Happens in Spiritual Direction?* Cincinnati, OH: Forward Movement, n.d. (Forward Movement pamphlets can be ordered at http://www.forwardmovement.org.)
- Henri J. Nouwen, *Spiritual Direction.* Cincinnati, OH: Forward Movement, 1981.

Articles

- Dennis Billy, "From Silence to Silence: The Spiritual Direction Session." *Presence* 8:2 (June 2002), 38-43. (Back issues of *Presence* can be ordered from Spiritual Directors International, http://www.sdiworld.org.)
- Linda Julian, "On Finding a Spiritual Director," http://www.osh.org/ministries/Ministries(LJarticle).html.
- Kathryn McCormick, "Seeking a Compass: Spiritual Directors Help Point the Way to a Deeper Relationship with God." http://www.episcopalchurch.org/episcopal-life/PrayDir.html.
- Gerald G. May, "Varieties of Spiritual Companionship." *Shalem News On Line* 22:1 (Winter 1998), http://www.shalem.org/sn/22.1gm.html.
- Shalem Institute, *Spiritual Direction: An Online Version of The Shalem Pamphlet on Spiritual Direction,* http://www.shalem.org/sd.html.

Organization

Spiritual Directors International
Post Office Box 25469
Seattle, WA 98125-2369
425-455-1565
http://www.sdiworld.org

Notes

1. Margaret Guenther, *Holy Listening: The Art of Spiritual Direction* (Cambridge, MA: Cowley Publications, 1992), 19–20.

2. Gerald G. May, *Care of Mind, Care of Spirit: A Psychiatrist Explores Spiritual Direction* (HarperSanFrancisco, 1992), 9.

3. Gordon H. Jeff, *Spiritual Direction for Every Christian* (London: SPCK, 1987), 99.

4. David E. Rosage, *Beginning Spiritual Direction* (Ann Arbor: Servant Publications, 1994), 51–52.

5. Ibid., 59.

6. Shalem Institute, *Spiritual Direction: An Online Version of The Shalem Pamphlet on Spiritual Direction,* http://www.shalem.org/sd.html.

7. Henri J. Nouwen, *Spiritual Direction* (Cincinnati, OH: Forward Movement, 1981), 10.

8. Alan Jones, *What Happens in Spiritual Direction?* (Cincinnati, OH: Forward Movement, n.d.), 3.

9. Shalem Institute, *Spiritual Direction: An Online Version of The Shalem Pamphlet on Spiritual Direction,* http://www.shalem.org/sd.html.

10. Gerald M. Fagin, "The Spirituality of the Spiritual Director," *Presence,* 8:3 (October 2002), 16.

11. Jones, *What Happens in Spiritual Direction?,* 7.

12. Ibid., 12.

13. Thomas M. Hedberg, Betsy Caprio, et. al, *A Code of Ethics for Spiritual Directors* (Pecos, NM: Dove Publications, 1992). Reprinted in this volume; see appendix 1.

CHAPTER TEN

Concluding Suggestions

When I first began to tell people that I was thinking of writing a book about ethics, boundaries, and transference in spiritual direction relationships, several of them reacted with rolls of the eyes or other indications that they wished I would choose a more exciting topic. There seems to be a belief abroad that interpersonal boundaries are boring, constricting, and inhibiting of spontaneity in relationships. But I disagree. I think setting boundaries and having guidelines that are carefully thought out in advance is ultimately freeing. Boundaries and guidelines give our directees a safe space in which to explore ideas and feelings they dare not discuss anywhere else, and they give us a reliable set of parameters within which we can allow our creativity—and, even more, God's—the room to operate. They free our directees to speak the truth without having to worry about the consequences, and they free us from having to make difficult decisions on the fly. They make it easier to have relationships that are at the same time intimate and safe.

OVERALL GUIDELINES

In doing research for this book, I surveyed a broad range of theories, insights, and opinions about interpersonal issues in helping relationships. I drew upon books, articles, Internet sites, tapes of convention sessions, peer supervision group meetings, conversations with other spiritual directors, and my own experiences with directees. From this body of information and experience I distilled the following array of suggestions or guidelines that I have come to find relevant and helpful to me as a spiritual director:

- Be honest with yourself. None of us is perfect, and we can get into trouble by trying to ignore or cover up areas where improvement is needed.
- Understand as much as possible about your own needs and personality dynamics. The more you know about yourself, the less likely you are to act out your issues inappropriately in the direction relationship.
- Learn how transference and countertransference operate. Understanding the power inherent in these processes reduces the probability that this power will be misused.
- Arrange your life so that your personal needs are met outside spiritual direction relationships.
- Even before problems arise, give thoughtful consideration to what you might do in the face of issues such as those discussed here. Ambivalent responses often make difficult situations worse,[1] and knowing where you stand in advance will leave room for more spontaneity. Furthermore, "mixed messages promote confusion. Especially for survivors of childhood abuse, for whom appropriate boundaries as children in relation to adults were nonexistent, predictable boundaries . . . are a priority for their healing. All persons in roles of leadership should convey clear messages about boundaries."[2]
- Build accountability into your support structure. That is, have reliable arrangements for supervision and for handling your own issues. Spiritual directors should not try to function in isolation.
- Learn to recognize when outside help is needed, and how and where to direct people to appropriate resources.
- Establish procedures for making ethical decisions in your direction relationships. Start by asking yourself, "Who is

most likely to benefit from what I am thinking of doing or saying?" and "Whose needs is this really meeting?" (see the following section).

* Establish a covenant at the outset of each direction relationship (see chapter 2).
* Remember always to involve God in your relationships and decision making!

ETHICAL DECISION MAKING

Virtually all codes of ethics have in common a vocabulary of virtue that includes terms like "competence," "confidentiality," "honesty," "respect," "responsibility," "integrity," "fairness," and "avoidance of exploitation." We might wonder whether it is not redundant to spell out how to manifest these qualities, if we are already firmly dedicated to the well-being of our directees. But even the most experienced and well-intentioned of us are not immune to misunderstanding, poor judgment, self-deception, or misuse of power. "The notion that 'if I do it, it isn't harmful because I am a good person and mean no harm' is a slippery slope of elitism that can lead any of us to elaborate rationalizations of our own behavior," asserted Marie Fortune.[3] "Sexually abusive therapists, for example, in almost all cases manage to convince themselves that their behavior is in the best interests of the patient," added Miriam Greenspan.[4]

One approach to making ethical decisions is to ask ourselves what our motives are and who is most likely to benefit from the actions in question. For example, Margaret Guenther described how she decides whether to disclose something about herself to a directee: "I ask myself: 'Why am I doing this? Will it help the directee? Or will my self-revelation be harmful, appropriating time, attention, and energy that rightly belong to the person sitting opposite me?'"[5] Likewise, Marie Fortune recommended considering questions such as the following in determining whether to relax boundaries in pastoral relationships: "What is the likely impact on or potential harm to the individual. . . ? Am I attempting to meet my needs at his or her expense?"[6]

Such an approach may occasionally fail to prevent us from making inappropriate choices, however. Decisions made on the basis of our own internal reasoning alone are not immune to the forces of self-deception alluded to by Miriam Greenspan's comment about sexually abusive therapists. Nor might those decisions be free from other sorts of errors or distortions. In the example in chapter 6, for instance, Dennis might well conclude that his plan to "rescue" Craig from his addiction to alcohol was plainly in Craig's best interest and had no self-serving component whatsoever.

I would suggest that an additional element of decision making, then, should be what Karen Lebacqz and Ronald Barton called a publicity test.[7] That is, we could stop to consider whether a cross section of reasonable adults would be likely to think a particular choice was appropriate. Or we could try to imagine (or better yet, seek out) the reactions of some people whose judgment we respect. For instance, if Alexandra in chapter 5 were to tell her peer supervision group she was thinking of suggesting to Bob that he might further his spiritual growth by taking some time away from the routine of his home life to go on a retreat with her, what would they say? "The test of publicity is designed to challenge privately held assumptions and hastily formed conclusions by requiring that arguments for one's position must survive the test of public scrutiny."[8] Such a test is not infallible (as evidenced, for example, in chapter 3 of Mark's gospel, where Jesus embarked on his ministry and his relatives and friends told him he must be crazy) and may tend to err on the side of caution, but its particular strength is that it moves decision making out of the idiosyncratic domain of the individual and into the wider arena of the community.

BOUNDARIES BUT NOT BARRIERS

Some of the authors in this area have expressed discomfort with the language of "boundaries," characterizing the concept of boundaries in helping relationships as hierarchical and artificially distancing (see chapters 4 and 5). But in the same article in which she challenged the "distance model" of psychotherapy, Miriam Greenspan suggested how interpersonal limits might be applied in a constructive way:

> The healing potential of psychotherapy has less to do with pseudo-objective distance than it does with safe connection. It is not about detached neutrality; it is about passionate but trustworthy engagement. . . .
>
> But what makes connection safe or trustworthy? And how do we cultivate safe connection? For me, the answers are largely a matter of . . . cultivating equality in a hierarchical relationship, mutuality in an inherently nonmutual relationship, empowerment in a power-imbalanced relationship. The therapist who sees himself as an all-knowing Expert and his client as a diagnosis is much more likely to abuse his power than the therapist who sees herself as an accountable coequal in therapy and her client as a person with an inherent wisdom that guides the therapeutic process.
>
> . . . Safe connection is about trustworthy companionship, not superior or omniscient power. And trustworthy companionship starts with an absolute and unshakable respect for the integrity of the person called patient or client.[9]

It seems to me that such a formula for trustworthy companionship would be highly applicable to the spiritual direction relationship, in which the directee is a healthy and competent participant and the only "superior or omniscient power" in the relationship is God.

Does it feel confining to function within a seemingly elaborate structure of guidelines like those suggested in this book? Not in my experience. On the contrary, I find such guidelines facilitative. Writing about boundaries in general, one author emphasized that "predictable and consistent boundaries of time, place, and all the rest serve to reduce anxiety and confusion in any given system, whether class, family, or church. They help establish an environment in which tough and difficult work can go on, work for which the outcome is less than certain. Their maintenance finally is honest and unselfish."[10] Another defined healthy relationships "as those which keep *boundaries* without creating *barriers*. . . . Those who set healthy boundaries are saying in essence, 'I will not be God to take care of your needs and I will not expect you to be God to take care of mine.'"[11] Paradoxically, creating a safe, predictable framework for our directees is what makes the spiritual direction relationship a place where we can explore with freedom and joy, and let God be God.

Notes

1. See, for example, Karen Lebacqz and Ronald G. Barton, "Boundaries, Mutuality, and Professional Ethics," in *Boundary Wars: Intimacy and Distance in Healing Relationships*, ed. Katherine Hancock Ragsdale (Cleveland: Pilgrim Press, 1996), 110, n. 30; and Bill Wallace, "Care of the Dying: *Power Between, Power Under,* and *Powerlessness With* as Means for Valuing and Balancing Boundaries and Mutuality," in *Boundary Wars*, 212.

2. Marie M. Fortune, "The Joy of Boundaries," in *Boundary Wars*, 83.

3. Ibid., 92.

4. Miriam Greenspan, "Out of Bounds," in *Boundary Wars*, 133.

5. Margaret Guenther, *Holy Listening: The Art of Spiritual Direction* (Cambridge, MA: Cowley Publications, 1992), 35; similarly, Ronald K. Bullis, *Sacred Calling, Secular Accountability: Law and Ethics in Complementary and Spiritual Counseling* (Philadelphia: Brunner-Routledge, 2001), 109–110.

6. Fortune, "Joy of Boundaries," 93.

7. Karen Lebacqz and Ronald G. Barton, *Sex in the Parish* (Louisville, KY: Westminster/John Knox Press, 1991), 42–67 passim.

8. Ibid., 53.

9. Greenspan, "Out of Bounds," 134.

10. Caroline Westerhoff, *Good Fences: The Boundaries of Hospitality* (Cambridge, MA: Cowley Publications, 1999), 90.

11. Thomas E. Rodgerson, *Spirituality, Stress and You* (New York: Paulist Press, 1994), 31.

A Code of Ethics for Spiritual Directors, Revised Edition

*Thomas M. Hedberg, S.D.B., and Betsy Caprio
and the staff of
The Center for Sacred Psychology*

Contents

IV. THE SPIRITUAL DIRECTION RELATIONSHIP
  A. Respect for the Freedom of Individual Conscience
  B. The Goal of Spiritual Development
  C. The Spiritual Direction Environment
  D. The Importance of Confidentiality
  E. Two Exceptions to the Rules of Confidentiality
  F. The Initial Spiritual Direction Meeting
  G. Periodic Evaluation of the Direction Relationship
  H. Termination

V. RELATIONSHIPS WITH OTHER PROFESSIONALS

VI. RELATIONSHIP TO THE COMMUNITY

Preface

In the absence of a national code of ethics for spiritual directors, the staff of the Center for Sacred Psychology in Los Angeles developed the following guidelines for its own use. We are a small network of spiritual guides and psychotherapists who focus on the relationship between Jungian psychology and spirituality. Among the Center staff contributing to this code were Cassi Bassolino, Audrey Bohan, Josie Broehm, Betsy Caprio, Michele Clark, Ruth Gerson, Thomas M. Hedberg, Barbra Hunter Duffy, Emmy Lee, Mary Betten Mitchell, Craig W. O'Neill, and Timothy G. Rawle. Other colleagues and advisors gave us their suggestions along the way.

Some of us have long-time associations with the School for Spiritual Directors at the Benedictine Abbey, Pecos, New Mexico. Editor Jim Scully of Dove Publications at Pecos believed our guidelines could be helpful to others engaged in the ministry of spiritual direction. Thus, Dove and the Center have collaborated on this first edition of a spiritual direction code of ethics. We hope it will help those of us who serve as spiritual directors reflect upon the fine points of this ever-expanding ministry, and also help to raise professional standards in the field.

One problem we encountered as we wrote was our own reluctance to become "legislative" about a ministry of love. We smiled a little ruefully when imagining what a desert mother or father might have to say about our efforts! However, the climate enveloping spiritual directors today in the United States—and, perhaps, throughout the world—is one which asks helpers in all fields to be very clear about their principles, their training, their motivation and their boundaries. In all helping professions, standards which protect the consumer are being raised, and much is being done to insure and maintain the high caliber of practitioners. Our hope is that guidelines for the spiritual director or companion, such as a non-binding code of ethics, will aid those of us involved in this beautiful ministry to serve the people of God even better.

In preparing this code, we have referred to the current professional statements of ethical principles of the following associations:

American Art Therapy Association
American Association for Counseling and Development
American Association for Marriage and Family Therapy
American Association of Pastoral Counselors
American Psychiatric Association (based on AMA code: i.e.,
    "Principles of Medical Ethics, with Annotations
    Especially Applicable to Psychiatry")
American Psychoanalytic Association
American Psychological Association
American School Counselor Association
California Association of Marriage and Family Therapists
Commission on Rehabilitation Counselor Certification
National Association of Social Workers
National Board for Certified Counselors
National Federation of Societies for Clinical Social Work
    with input also from guidelines of the Association of
    Christian Therapists and the Christian Legal Society

This code of ethics is just a start. Its creators welcome comments and reactions to it, with an eye to refining the code in further editions. Please send any reactions and suggestions to the

Center for Sacred Psychology
Box 643 Gateway Station
Culver City, CA 90232 (310/838-0279)

I. STATEMENT OF PURPOSE

A. The Nature of Spiritual Direction

Spiritual direction is an ancient ministry, a unique one-to-one relationship in which a trained person assists another person in the search for an ever-closer union of love with God. Both lay and ordained women and men practice this ministry today, as in the past. In a spiritual direction partnership, both persons share a belief in the reality of the spiritual and agree that relationship to this spiritual realm is life's primary purpose.

Traditionally, spiritual directors meet regularly (usually monthly) with those coming to share their journeys of faith. Directors do not impose their own wills or agendas on others; rather, they listen carefully to the unfolding of directees' lives, so as to help them discern the ways in which God is leading them.

B. Terminology

Although the term "spiritual director" is used throughout this code, it is a term with limitations. Other expressions, such as "spiritual companion," "spiritual friend, "soul friend" and "spiritual guide," highlight different aspects of the relationship. Since "spiritual director" is the traditional term and the one most people use today, it is retained—but in its fullest sense, incorporating the nuances of its synonyms. A review of the literature in this field shows that most contemporary spiritual directors are *not* very directive.

Traditionally, those receiving direction are spoken of as "directees," and so this term is also retained.

The language of this code is as inclusive as possible, making it suitable for spiritual directors of all faiths. Denominational statements (e.g., Christian, Jewish, etc.) would be more specific, of course.

C. Purpose of This Code

This code is similar to the professional codes of other ministries and helping professions, yet reflects the differences unique to the *three*-way relationship that is spiritual direction. "Whenever two . . . come together in My Name, there too am I" (Mt. 18:20).

Ethical behavior results not from edict, of course, but from personal commitment. The purpose of a statement such as this code is threefold:

1. To provide norms for ethical spiritual direction and for the training and continuing education of directors.
2. To have a checklist for those engaged in this ministry which can be used for prayer and reflection.
3. To present norms to those who come for spiritual direction so they will know the director's standards, especially at a time when public accountability from those in ministry is more needed than ever.

II. THE SPIRITUAL DIRECTOR'S QUALITIES AND TRAINING

The following represents an ideal towards which the spiritual director may aim. Since development in any ministry is gradual, these goals are not meant to discourage or produce anxiety for those of us who are not yet perfect!

A. Directors Answer and Nurture a Call to This Ministry

Those offering to be spiritual directors for others believe their ministry to be a gift from God. They are responding to an inner call, sent in answer to their own prayer about how God wishes to use them. The inner attraction towards this ministry is confirmed externally when they discover that others seek them out for counsel.

Therefore, spiritual directors know that their own ongoing life of prayer and relationship to God is the most important gift they bring to those who come to them for spiritual direction. They have been in spiritual direction (and, often, therapy and/or analysis) for several years and see the commitment to their own spiritual development as a lifelong process. They are dedicated travelers on the interior pathways.

B. Directors Receive Training

Spiritual directors receive training before embarking on this ministry, and are happy to discuss this training with those seeking guidance. Spiritual directors are also willing to speak of their own spiritual background, leanings and preferences when this is appropriate.

Directors are familiar with the historical roots of their ministry in the various religious traditions of the world. This background gives contemporary spiritual directors a sense of their heritage and an appreciation of those who have gone before.

As much as possible, spiritual directors are continually engaged in furthering their competency in both theoretical and applied spiritual theology, as well as in the many adjunctive fields of study which enhance this ministry, such as scripture, comparative religion, psychology, folklore, the arts, popular culture, and even the sciences. Professional growth, like personal, continues for a lifetime.

Spiritual directors know, however, that their ministry is an art, not the fruit of learning alone. They agree with C. G. Jung's advice: "Learn your theories as well as you can, but put them aside when you touch the miracle of the living soul" (quoted in *Psychological Reflections*, p. 84).

C. Directors Develop Healthy Relationships

Spiritual directors are aware of the importance of a personal emotional support system, and do whatever they need to do to develop such support. It is by having friendship and intimacy needs met outside of spiritual direction relationships that they are best able to assure their directees of objectivity and freedom from any of their own hidden (and usually unconscious) emotional agendas.

D. Directors Guard Their Health

Spiritual directors understand the causes of stress and burnout in ministry. Among these are over-scheduling, too many directees, and too little prayer and reflection time before and after sessions.

Directors carefully guard their physical and emotional well-being, as well as their spiritual health, monitoring and taking preventive measures to protect these. Wise directors know that stress in themselves is detrimental to those coming for assistance and that a large part of being a "playable instrument for God" depends upon their own fitness.

E. Directors Receive Supervision

Spiritual directors augment their skills and objectivity by seeking supervision from other experienced directors when this is appropriate and possible. Supervisors should be chosen for their respect for the human soul as well as for their knowledge and experience. They should not be in any position of authority over the directees whose material will be shared with them.

Supervision involves consultation about issues and problems encountered while engaged in this ministry. One can never reach a degree of excellence that makes supervision no longer necessary.

Supervisors need to be aware of directors' standards regarding confidentiality (see Section IV E, below) and agree to the same level of silence about material brought to supervision. As much as possible, the identity of those being discussed in supervision is disguised, and specifics of particular cases reframed as broader issues.

Group or peer supervision requires special attention to the maintenance of confidentiality.

F. Directors Value Professional Sharing

Professional sharing among spiritual directors in the same geographical area is a valuable adjunct to this ministry, as is membership in professional associations, such as Spiritual Directors International (2300 Adeline Dr., Burlingame, CA 94010). In this way, directors can keep abreast of developments in their field and have a forum in which to discuss issues bearing on their ministry.

III. SPIRITUAL DIRECTION BOUNDARIES

A. Distinctions between Spiritual Direction and Other Helping Professions

Spiritual directors understand the boundaries of spiritual direction, and how it is different from pastoral counseling, psychotherapy, analysis, or a prayer-partner relationship in which persons share equally (see Tilden Edwards, *Spiritual Friend*, p. 130ff). Directors strive to clarify this distinction for directees.

Wise spiritual directors continually remind themselves of the purpose of spiritual direction and of how easily it can slide into the style of counseling. They guard against such shifting by continually reflecting on the truth that it is God who is the Director. By preparing for sessions with prayer and by reviewing sessions, asking if these were focused on God in the directee's life, they are able to maintain the uniqueness of spiritual direction. A single-hearted vision about these relationships, as well as praying with and for directees, will enable spiritual directors to remain within their ministry's boundaries.

Both to preserve the character of spiritual direction, and also to avoid infringing upon the terrain of the psychotherapist, directors use psychological tools that enhance self-knowledge (such as the Myers-Briggs Type Indicator) with care. They offer such instruments to directees only after receiving training in their use, with due respect for the areas of soul which may be opened up by them, and with awareness of the possible abuses to which their superficial use can lead (e.g., labeling, "typecasting," etc.).

Training is also a prerequisite for spiritual directors offering specialized adjunctive aids such as bodywork, art and sand tray experiences, role playing, inner healing techniques, the Enneagram, and any of the many other valuable ways of stirring the soul that have roots in both psychology and spirituality. Testing instruments designed for psychological diagnosis (such as the MMPI and MCMI) are outside the scope of spiritual direction.

Spiritual directors will want to reflect carefully on the growing tendency in their field to adopt terminology and practices from the world of psychology. This interface between the two disciplines which deal with the human soul or psyche is often of the greatest help; the pitfall, however, is that the unique nature of spiritual direction can be swallowed up by the psychologist's clinical language and points of view (see Section IV D). When this happens, the purpose and value of spiritual direction is diminished, and the spiritual director may turn into someone practicing analysis or psychotherapy without a license (which is unethical).

In addition to spiritual direction and the highly trained professions rooted in various psychologies, there also exist today several sorts of non-regulated one-to-one relationships focusing on human development and faith experience. Among these are types of faith healing and prayer ministry. It is important for spiritual directors to distinguish clearly, both for themselves and directees, the differences between their ministry and these other practices which may bear some resemblance to it. Two major distinctions can be noted:

1. Spiritual direction is an ongoing relationship with regularly scheduled meetings between the director and the person coming for guidance. A verbal (or, sometimes, written) contract to this effect is made between the two parties. This is different from seeking out a helper on an as-needed basis.
2. Spiritual direction centers on how material brought to the session *by the directee* reflects the presence of God in that person's life. The directee is considered the more active member of the partnership; the director's role is to listen, question, suggest, rephrase, offer resources and, of course, pray with and for the directee. As Morton Kelsey writes, "The basic meaning of spiritual guidance is to stand by people in their seeking and searching . . . " (*Companions on the Inner Way*, p. 59). There is a difference between coming for spiritual direction and the more passive stance adopted when requesting another to pray over one or to give one advice.

These distinctions are not made to reflect negatively on those engaged in other ministries which resemble spiritual direction, but to clarify the particular nature of the latter.

B. Referrals to Counselors, Psychologists, Psychotherapists and Psychiatrists

Spiritual directors recognize those occasions when the limits of spiritual direction are breached. For such times, they have on hand and use referrals to competent (and, if possible, spiritually-oriented) psychotherapists and others. Directors should have more than one referral to offer, if possible, and should assure the directee of continued support in whatever way is deemed best by the primary helper (now, the licensed doctor, therapist or therapy intern; see Section V). *Directees are never to be abandoned.*

On the other hand, directors should not agree to continue as the sole helping person for someone who obviously needs psychological help and refuses to seek it upon such recommendation. To do so may prevent the person in need of aid from reaching out for it "because I have a spiritual director."

Some spiritual directors also have training as pastoral counselors or psychotherapists, so that they themselves can move into a therapeutic stance when appropriate. In such cases, directors will want to be very clear with directees about the shift to a therapist-client relationship, while continuing to include in sessions the spiritual dimension of their original relationship.

C. Choice of Directees

Spiritual directors may choose with whom to work. They know the maximum number of persons whom they can see while still maintaining serenity, and do not exceed this number.

In addition, directors do not think it possible to be of help to everyone, and discerningly screen prospective directees. (For example, directors trained in the Ignatian method may choose not to work with those seeking a Jungian or a charismatic approach to the soul; directors with an unfinished personal issue may choose not to take on a directee with a similar issue.)

Spiritual directors have a heightened consciousness of ecumenical, ethnic, and gender-related issues, as well as other contemporary concerns. When aware of biases or prejudices on their own part, they try to attend to them. Directors do not discriminate among potential directees because of gender, age, economic status, religion, physical challenges, marital status, political belief, sexual/affectional orientation, race, national origin or ethnicity. However, directors may choose not to work with such directees for other, non-discriminatory reasons, including a lack of understanding of their particular needs. (For example, a young spiritual director might feel unable to minister well to an elderly directee; a heterosexual director may be unversed in or uncomfortable with issues concerning gay and lesbian directees.)

Wise directors, then, are aware of their lack of familiarity with certain styles of spirituality or with particular aspects of life, of their own biases, and of their unresolved personal issues which may affect direction. If necessary, they are also able to speak honestly of these to potential directees. At the same time, believing that God is also involved in any request for direction, spiritual directors do not lightly turn a person away and, if they do so, attempt to help that person find a suitable director.

Spiritual direction is traditionally effected in person. Some directors are open to direction via letters and/or tapes in the mail, or by telephone conversation. "Long-distance direction" may be called for when a directee has moved away, or when someone cannot find suitable direction in their own area; it has a firm place in the history of this ministry. While the in-person relationship is always to be preferred and recommended, directors should consider their policy on working with others at a distance, as well as on the occasional phone session with regular directees.

D. Dual Relationships

Dual relationships (commonly described as mixed roles or "wearing more than one hat") need to be carefully evaluated. Prohibited, of course, is any covert or overt sexual intimacy or involvement between the two parties, or between the director and a directee's spouse or partner.

Other types of dual relationships include socializing or business dealings with directees, direction relationships which flower into two-way friendships, bartering or exchanges of services, spiritual direction with one's friends, family members, students or supervisees, and directing close friends or more than one person from the same family. Most codes of ethics for the helping professions have clear strictures against such role-mixing, strictures wisely designed to safeguard the boundaries of the client's contained space. Spiritual directors are well-advised to give serious consideration to this norm.

However, in spiritual direction dual relationships are not automatically prohibited, as this partnership has another dimension: it has a three-way nature which includes a God with a long history of breaking rules! The chronicles of spiritual direction are noteworthy for the numbers of "multiple hats" people have worn, often out of necessity (e.g., being both teacher and director).

Rather than following a legalistic set of minute rules about dual relationships, directors should use common sense, seeking mutual understanding between themselves and directees in the face of possible overlaps. The primary goal is to ensure a "clean" space for spiritual direction, while still allowing the Spirit to move freely; the touchstone is that any mixing of roles not compromise the effectiveness of the spiritual direction relationship. The ancient maxim of the healing arts—"Above all, do no harm"—applies well to this aspect of spiritual direction.

With consciousness and dialogue as the keys, there can be verbal acknowledgment of any shifting of roles, if and when this happens and, if possible, separation of any other activities between the two persons from the spiritual direction site and time.

E. Physical Boundaries in Spiritual Direction

In addition to avoiding any sexual intimacy with directees, spiritual directors should consciously examine their position on physical contact with those who come to them, being sensitive to this as a plus or a minus in each relationship.

They need to be aware of their own motives for touching, directees' cultural attitudes toward touch, timing and types of such contacts, and whether or not they restrict touch to those of the same or the opposite gender.

Holding hands to pray, healing touch, and amiable embraces

are all acceptable and natural, and can be most helpful in the spiritual direction partnership. Directors, however, should *consciously*—not accidentally—participate in such actions; they ask whether these promote or take away from the overall purpose of each relationship, rather than indiscriminately imposing them on directees. Neither does the wise director automatically consent to physical contact initiated by a directee without evaluating its benefit or detriment to their joint goal.

F. Psychological Boundaries in Spiritual Direction

Spiritual directors understand the psychological issues that most often arise when two souls meet intimately, and know how to deal with them. Primary among these are issues of transference (the projection of unconscious feelings and material in the directee onto the director) and countertransference (the projection of unconscious feelings and material in the director onto the directee).

Directors are well aware that their own needs will be constellated continually by these direction relationships; they try to remain conscious of these needs to the best of their abilities, so as not to get in God's way or interfere with grace. On the other hand, directors know that such a continuous level of awareness is never completely possible, and they are able to accept their own human shortcomings with humility—and, if at all possible, with humor!

Two particular areas of "leaky margins" are:

1. Sessions that become filled with the director's own material: e.g., anecdotes, news, feelings, etc. Some such self-disclosure may be appropriate and very useful when done consciously, as it offers examples, and helps to create a bond between the two persons, but directors must always remember that the soul-life of the directee is the focus of their time together.

2. Giving and receiving of gifts. Directees not infrequently bring tokens of appreciation and affection to their guides; spiritual directors may also wish to give small remembrances to directees, especially when they find a picture, book or other item bearing on their joint work.

Such exchanges are certainly natural in a close relationship;

they are not inappropriate in spiritual direction (as they might be in therapy), *unless* they in some way compromise the objectivity of the director or the freedom of the directee. (Examples of compromising gifts would be very expensive or very personal items that have "obligation" written all over them.)

IV. THE SPIRITUAL DIRECTION RELATIONSHIP

In addition to the boundaries indicated in Section III, the following guidelines are recommended:

A. Respect for the Freedom of Individual Conscience

This is a cornerstone of authentic spiritual guidance. The director is to be companion and reflector, not "Big Brother" or "Answer Lady." Dependency is never to be encouraged.

Directors do not have their own agendas and expectations for directees—other than the broad goal of a closer walk with God—but seek with each person to discern God's unique and sacred plan in that person's life. Directors accept directees as they are. They respect others' religious convictions and never proselytize for their own religious denomination or theological or psychological points of view, even though they are willing to be appropriately open about their own commitment to these (e.g., particular forms of prayer, tithing, the Twelve Steps, etc.).

Curiosity or "intellectual voyeurism" should not be a motivating factor in the ministry of spiritual direction; the director asks personal questions only if these contribute to directees' deepening awareness of God in their lives. Ethical directors avoid "spiritual safecracking": that is, the probing attitude of some aggressive styles of therapy.

B. The Goal of Spiritual Development

Spiritual growth is not solely introspective, but also involves the overflowing of God's life in a person into a needy world. The spiritual director encourages this balance between "contemplation and sharing with others the fruits of contemplation" (as the motto of the Dominican order has it) in the lives of those coming for direction.

C. The Spiritual Direction Environment

Spiritual direction sessions should take place in an environment of privacy, peacefulness and safety. Soundproofing and wheelchair access are recommended. Direction sessions should be faithful to their appointed hours. The ideal is that the period of spiritual direction be a protected time, a "Sabbath-time," in a nourishing, oasis-like space that speaks to the directee of first priorities.

It is not only the setting but also the demeanor of the director which contributes to this sense of *temenos* or sacred set-apartness. When coming for spiritual direction, directees should be able to trust that their time is dedicated to them. As well as they can, spiritual directors guard against intrusions and interruptions by other persons and phone calls. The director also avoids "shop-talk" with the directee which meets the director's needs.

D. The Importance of Confidentiality

Confidentiality is essential; the person coming to direction must be able to count on it. Without the informed consent and written permission of the directee, the director may not disclose verbally or in writing *any* information (no matter how insignificant) learned in current or past spiritual direction sessions. This stricture also applies to a directee's art work or other visual expression, and covers the release of information to other helpers in the directee's life, such as therapists. Clerical spiritual directors in some faith traditions are bound by the seal of confession or an equivalent to this. Although non-clerical spiritual directors (as well as clerical directors seeing directees outside of sacramental confession) are not bound by the seal of confession, their attitude toward the sacred trust placed in them is to be the same.

Spiritual directors do not reveal the names of those whom they serve in this capacity, past or present, nor do they allude to them in conversation (even anonymously as "a sister" or "someone who comes to me for direction"). On the other hand, because the shared relationship is one which gives glory to God, neither party need feel they must conceal it by extraordinary means for protecting anonymity, such as separate entrances and exits, or by pretending other people in a waiting area are invisible!

In fact, the paths of persons working with the same spiritual director may often cross; they share something precious which need not be disguised, but may well be celebrated. The director might mention to persons coming for direction the possibility that they will encounter others who come to the same site, just to preclude surprises.

Directees should also be encouraged to maintain reticence about the content of sessions, out of respect for the sacredness of the interior life. Such a stance protects and contains the directee's inner world; it is thus less easily diffused and intruded upon. This is, however, a recommendation to the person seeking guidance and is not obligatory (as is the director's confidentiality).

Spiritual direction notes and files should be stored in a way that insures confidentiality. Nothing should be put in writing which would be against the directee's best interest in the unlikely event that notes should ever be made public. Directors should make some provision, in advance, for the safe disposal of all such notes and files at the time of their retirement or death.

Taping (audio or video) of sessions by the director for any reason is strongly discouraged, not only for reasons of confidentiality but also because taping adds an inappropriate clinical tone to spiritual direction. If taping does occur, it should be for some unusual reason only, and with the directee's full foreknowledge and written consent for each taped session. Directees have the option of taping sessions for their own later reviews.

Spiritual direction case studies for teaching, writing or other public purposes should be, ideally, facsimiles. In the event that verbatim accounts of actual sessions are used for teaching, this may be done only with the *written* consent of the directee, and should be used to that person's advantage. (For example, a directee could help to prepare the presentation, which would offer a valuable chance to review the direction experience.) However, it is advised that this sort of request to make sacred material public not be included in spiritual direction except for exceptional reasons; there are alternative, less clinical, ways of teaching and writing about spiritual direction. The same reservations apply to research in this field, including third party observations of sessions.

The underlying principles at work in these cautions about recording and presenting direction material is the need to demonstrate the greatest possible reverence for the soul. The practices advised against are not wrong and are, in fact, widely used to advantage in other helping professions; still, many feel they are less-than-optimum ways of showing respect for the intimate, sacred content of spiritual direction. Attentive care to such matters does credit to the integrity both of directors and of those who trust them, and is a constant reminder to all of the unique nature of this ministry. A directee is not a clinical case.

Directors who practice group spiritual direction are bound by the same rules of confidentiality as for individual sessions. They also receive written commitments from group members to respect the norms of confidentiality and, at intervals during the group's life, remind members of this obligation.

E. Two Exceptions to the Rules of Confidentiality

1. Spiritual directors often seek supervision as a valued adjunct to their ministry (see Section II E). They are to inform directees of this fact and of the mode and frequency of supervision, assuring them that material brought to supervision is kept as anonymous as possible. Directees who have any objection to a director's policies about supervision must have their wishes respected.

2. Should directees report anything which involves serious harm to themselves, or to another, a director is bound in conscience to work out some way to intervene, *particularly if the endangered person is a minor*. This provision also applies to so-called "third-party reports" (i.e., the directee reveals knowledge of danger to others).

Legal requirements are related to but distinguished from ethical standards. Non-licensed counselors (including spiritual directors) are not mandated by law to report cases of potential suicide, but surely have a moral duty to refer suicidal persons to mental health professionals and to be sure that referrals are acted upon. It is also strongly recommended that a director in such a situation contact family members of the person at risk, preferably with that person's cooperation.

In cases where there is clear danger to another's safely or life (e.g. child abuse), spiritual directors, like all citizens, have a duty to warn the endangered parties or their legal guardians, and are morally responsible to intervene by reporting such danger to the proper authorities. Directors who are also licensed therapists or therapist-interns are, in most states, mandated by law to report, and must obey this law with anyone seeing them for direction as well as with therapy clients. Spiritual directors will want to become familiar with state regulations which apply to them; local networks of directors might make research on this topic a high priority, perhaps with help from local clergy.

A spiritual director should *never* be party to the physical or psychological damage of another person, nor to any covering-up of such damage no matter how powerful the authority of anyone or any institution which might wish to conceal such actions. At the same time, while justice has the highest priority, the spiritual director also will want to avoid scandal and damage to others' reputations wherever possible. The ministry of spiritual director is not that of religious vigilante or watchdog.

Whenever possible, intervention and prevention should come from the person receiving direction, backed up by the director. The director can explore any action which needs to be taken in light of the other's search for a closer relationship with God. Directees should understand that even though spiritual direction is not legally considered a privileged communication, the director's first obligation is always to the directee, not to institutions or other collectives. Directors are on the side of those coming to them for guidance.

F. The Initial Spiritual Direction Meeting

A first session between a spiritual director and a person seeking direction is exploratory in nature, with attention to the following:

- the needs, readiness, hopes and expectations of the potential directee
- religious beliefs
- the biases, values, and styles of both parties
- discernment about the compatibility of the person seeking direction with the particular director's point of view, training, skills and experience
- available resources (e.g.: books and tapes for loan)
- agreement on the frequency of meetings as well as remuneration, if any
- necessity of and plans for ongoing evaluation
- policies on the director's availability by phone and on cancellations
- the director's commitment of time and prayer to directees
- the directee's past experience with spiritual direction, and with any counseling modalities (see Section V)
- standards of confidentiality and supervision of the director (see Section IV E).

Directors may choose at this time to have those beginning direction sign a release saying the director (church, retreat center, etc.) will not be held responsible for any physical injury, property loss or damage which may occur to directees (or anyone accompanying them) while at the site of spiritual direction.

It is also recommended that the inquirer be advised of the code of ethics to which the director subscribes, whether this one or some other, and offered some means of perusing it at length.

The initial meeting should also include an opportunity for the potential directee to ask questions of the director.

G. Periodic Evaluation of the Direction Relationship

Regular evaluation times (every six months or so), in which both parties discern whether or not the relationship is to continue, are important. The guideline for the director is, always, freedom for the person coming for assistance. One must never cling to directees but, rather, try to find ways to ease the termination process if this is indicated by God's movement in the other's heart.

A helpful guideline for evaluation is whether or not the spiritual direction relationship is bearing fruit in a directee's life. The two can examine together the nature of these fruits. Another simple touchstone for evaluation is a comparison of the directee's spiritual life as it was when the relationship began with the way it is now: "How were you praying then?" and "Has that changed?" and "Does this seem like a positive change?" are useful questions.

H. Termination

Spiritual direction relationships end for various reasons. The director has the responsibility of bringing the relationship to a satisfactory completion, perhaps with a ritual or ceremony and/or a review of the time shared.

Endings to a direction relationship are best effected over several sessions, out of respect for the specialness of the joint work that has been done and so that the directee has time to make alternative arrangements. If the termination is abrupt, the director will still endeavor to find some way to effect completion—a final session is preferable, in lieu of which a closing letter or, at least, a phone call, is better than an open-ended rending of a sacred bond.

When directors terminate, they make every effort to prevent other persons from feeling abandoned. The bond of trust undertaken when one agrees to be a spiritual director should not be broken lightly or abruptly.

When directees terminate, directors freely and graciously release them with no attempt at dissuasion.

A director may wish to assure a departing directee of future remembrance in prayer. Once made, such an assurance is to be considered an ongoing responsibility.

V. RELATIONSHIPS WITH OTHER PROFESSIONALS

Spiritual directors refrain from disparagement of others in any of the helping professions. They recognize the value of different points of view in the many companioning types of work, and understand and respect the religious plurality of our society.

Spiritual directors generously make themselves and their expertise available to others discerning a call to this ministry, deeming it a privilege to share the fruits of their training and experience. They are committed to the development of the ministry of spiritual direction, and to the raising of professional standards among directors.

When someone comes for spiritual direction, the director will ask if the person is seeing anyone for counseling or psychotherapy at this time. If this is the case, the directee should be asked to clear the spiritual direction arrangement with this other person (pastoral counselor, analyst, psychotherapist, etc.), and to get a written acknowledgment of the addition of spiritual direction to the original helper's treatment plan. A form letter may be used for such purposes; this is not the same as a release of information form. This guideline is included, primarily, as an ethical courtesy to other professionals, but also provides legal protection for the director in the unlikely event that it should be needed.

Spiritual directors should also ask directees to inform them if they enter psychotherapy or analysis during their time of spiritual direction, and follow the same procedure for contacting the other professional.

Potential directees need to have terminated with one spiritual director before beginning with another.

VI. RELATIONSHIP TO THE COMMUNITY

Traditionally, spiritual directors have not publicized or advertised their services, or promoted themselves in other ways. They do not solicit or recruit directees. Parish or temple staffs, schools, or other places which employ spiritual directors, such as diocesan offices or retreat centers, will make it known that spiritual direction is one of the services offered. Spiritual directors who work independently usually find that directees come to them through word of mouth.

Spiritual directors may have professional cards (or flyers describing their work) to distribute to those who request them.

These should be completely factual, making no claims or promises about the fruits of spiritual direction or about the director's effectiveness. In addition, spiritual directors make no verbal or written "guarantees" about the results of their ministry (e.g., "Come and be healed!").

Spiritual directors stand ready, when necessary, to render service to others in need of their expertise. Directors who receive remuneration for their time often reserve a percentage of reduced-fee or no-fee appointments for those who would not be able to see them otherwise. It is recommended that such directors decide which group(s) of persons come under this heading (e.g.: the sick, the dying, the homeless, elderly religious, those who live with/minister to the poor, etc.), and that they share this information with all who come to them, as the financial contributions of some help to subsidize the others.

Directors are as clear as possible, when describing their ministry, about its distinction from other one-to-one helping professions. They are careful not to fall into the use of protected terminology, such as "psychologist," "counselor," or "therapist"; for example, spiritual directors may not refer to themselves as "prayer therapists."

Finally, spiritual directors strive, by the way they live, to be good representatives of their ministry.

Although it is extremely useful to members of the helping professions to have codes of ethics detailing the practice of their work or ministry, spiritual directors in particular will want to stay focused on how their purpose goes far beyond rules and regulations. The binding force behind this code comes not from words on paper, but from each spiritual director's ever-developing relationship with God. No one of us may live up to all that is written here—but, if we err, let it be on the side of love.

Spiritual Directors International
Guidelines for Ethical Conduct

ETHICAL GUIDELINES TASK FORCE:

Lucy Abbott-Tucker
Roman Catholic/Chicago, IL USA
Staff Member, Institute for Spiritual Leadership

Bill Creed, SJ
Roman Catholic/Chicago, IL USA
Director, Ignatian Spirituality Project

Andrew Dreitcer, MDiv, PhD
Presbyterian/Claremont, CA USA
Associate Professor of Spirituality
Director of Spiritual Formation
Claremont School of Theology

Richard M. Gula, SS
Roman Catholic/Berkeley, CA USA
Professor of Moral Theology
Franciscan School of Theology

Joyce McFarland
Episcopal/Collegeville, MN USA
Chair of the Board
Institute for Ecumenical and Social Research

Timothy E. O'Connell, PhD
Roman Catholic/Chicago, IL USA
Professor of Christian Ethics
Loyola University Chicago

Dorothy Whiston
Roman Catholic/Iowa City, IA USA
Founder, Soul Friends Ecumenical Ministry

The History of Spiritual Directors International

Spiritual Directors International [SDI] is an ecumenical association of colleagues, grounded in the Christian faith, whose sole purpose is to serve the growing network of spiritual directors worldwide and the people who train them. The inspiration for this network began in 1989 at Mercy Center in Burlingame, California, USA.

Spiritual Directors International Mission Statement

Throughout human history individuals have been called to accompany others seeking the Mystery we name God. In this time, Spiritual Directors International responds to this call by tending the holy around the world and across traditions.

Adoption Resolution

"There is unanimous consensus by the Coordinating Council that these are the official Guidelines for Ethical Conduct of Spiritual Directors International. It is our joy to promulgate these guidelines for distribution. We hope that our colleagues will strive to accept these as their personal guidelines."

— *adopted by Spiritual Directors International Coordinating Council, March 30, 1999*

GUIDELINES FOR ETHICAL CONDUCT

Ethical conduct flows from lived reverence for God, self, and others but is not inevitably the reality of every spiritual direction relationship. Therefore, these guidelines are meant to inspire members of Spiritual Directors International toward integrity, responsibility, and faithfulness in their practice of spiritual direction.

I. THE SPIRITUAL DIRECTOR AND THE SELF

Personal Spirituality

1. Spiritual directors assume responsibility for personal growth by:
   a. participating in regular spiritual direction
   b. following personal and communal spiritual practices and disciplines.

Formation

2. Spiritual directors engage in ongoing formation as directors by:
   a. continuing to discern their call to the ministry of spiritual direction
   b. nurturing self-knowledge and freedom
   c. cultivating insight into the influences of culture, social-historical context, environmental setting, and institutions
   d. studying scripture, theology, spirituality, and other disciplines related to spiritual direction.

Supervision

3. Spiritual directors engage in supervision by:
   a. receiving regular supervision from peers or from a mentor
   b. seeking consultations with other appropriately qualified persons when necessary.

Personal Responsibility

4. Spiritual directors meet their needs outside the spiritual direction relationship in a variety of ways, especially by:
   a. self care, wisely balancing time for worship, work, leisure, family, and personal relationships

b. addressing the difficulties multiple roles or relationships pose to the effectiveness or clarity of the spiritual direction relationship

c. removing oneself from any situation that compromises the integrity of the spiritual direction relationship.

Limitations

5. Spiritual directors recognize the limits of:
   a. energy by restricting the number of directees
   b. attentiveness by appropriate spacing of meetings and directees
   c. competence by referring directees to other appropriately qualified persons when necessary.

II. THE SPIRITUAL DIRECTOR AND THE DIRECTEE

Covenant

1. Spiritual directors initiate conversation and establish agreements with directees about:
   a. the nature of spiritual direction
   b. the roles of the director and the directee
   c. the length and frequency of direction sessions
   d. the compensation, if any, to be given to the director or institution
   e. the process for evaluating and terminating the relationship.

Dignity

2. Spiritual directors honor the dignity of the directee by:
   a. respecting the directee's values, conscience, spirituality, and theology
   b. inquiring into the motives, experiences, or relationships of the directee only as necessary
   c. recognizing the imbalance of power in the spiritual direction relationship and taking care not to exploit it
   d. establishing and maintaining appropriate physical and psychological boundaries with the directee

e. refraining from sexualizing behavior, including, but not limited to, manipulative, abusive, or coercive words or actions toward a directee.

Confidentiality
3. Spiritual directors maintain the confidentiality and the privacy of the directee by:
   a. protecting the identity of the directee
   b. keeping confidential all oral and written matters arising in the spiritual direction sessions
   c. conducting direction sessions in appropriate settings
   d. addressing legal regulations requiring disclosure to proper authorities, including but not limited to, child abuse, elder abuse, and physical harm to self and others.

III. THE SPIRITUAL DIRECTOR AND OTHERS
Colleagues
1. Spiritual directors maintain collegial relationships with ministers and professionals by:
   a. developing intra- and interdisciplinary relationships
   b. requesting a directee who is in therapy to inform his or her therapist about being in spiritual direction
   c. securing written releases and permission from directees when specific information needs to be shared for the benefit of the directee
   d. respecting ministers and professionals by not disparaging them or their work.

Faith Communities
2. Spiritual directors maintain responsible relationships to communities of faith by:
   a. remaining open to processes of corporate discernment, accountability, and support
   b. appropriately drawing on the teachings and practices of communities of faith

c. respecting the directee's relationship to his or her own community of faith.

Society

3. Spiritual directors, when presenting themselves to the public, preserve the integrity of spiritual direction by:
   a. representing qualifications and affiliations accurately
   b. defining the particular nature and purpose of spiritual direction
   c. respecting all persons regardless of race, color, sex, sexual orientation, age, religion, national origin, marital status, political belief, mental or physical handicap, any preference, personal characteristic, condition or status.

For Reflection

Spiritual Directors International recognizes that cultural and environmental factors may require these guidelines to be contextualized for different types of spiritual direction experiences. Spiritual Directors International encourages individuals, training programs, religious institutions, healthcare systems, spirituality centers, supervision circles and regional Spiritual Directors International groups to review and re-appropriate these guidelines. To facilitate dialogue and re-appropriation of these guidelines, Spiritual Directors International offers these questions for reflection:

a. How do you and your community define terms such as "spiritual direction," "formation," and "supervision"?
b. How do you and your community understand potential difficulties associated with "multiple roles and relationships," "imbalance of power," "boundaries," and "confidentiality"?
c. How might the various guidelines contribute to the authenticity of your practice of spiritual direction? Your community's practice of spiritual direction?
d. How might you adapt these guidelines in your particular cultural or institutional setting?
e. What ethical concerns in spiritual direction do you and your community foresee that these guidelines do not address?

Annotated Bibliography

Note: Internet addresses often change without notice. Such addresses included here are accurate as of the time they were last accessed during the preparation of this book.

Codes of Ethics and Policy Statements

American Association of Pastoral Counselors. *Code of Ethics.* http://www.aapc.org/ethics.htm. Amended April 28, 1994. Accessed March 3, 2001.

American Counseling Association. *ACA Code of Ethics and Standards of Practice.* http://www.counseling.org/site/PageServer?pagename= resources_ethics#ce. Revised 1995. Accessed January 8, 2001.

American Psychoanalytic Association. *Principles and Standards of Ethics for Psychoanalysts.* http://www.apsa.org/ethics901.htm. Revised September 24, 2001. Accessed January 9, 2002.

American Psychological Association. *Ethical Principles of Psychologists and Code of Conduct.* Washington, DC: American Psychological Association, 1992.

Episcopal Diocese of New York. *Sexual Misconduct in the Church: What Are the Rules and How It Is Handled.* http://www.dioceseny.org/convention/pbook/misconduct.htm#1. Accessed June 13, 2002.

Episcopal Diocese of Southern Ohio. *Policy and Definition of Sexual Misconduct.* http://www.episcopalian.org/dsoyouth/guide/ paperwork/Misconduct.html. Accessed June 13, 2002.

Hedberg, Thomas M., Betsy Caprio, and the Staff of The Center for Sacred Psychology. *A Code of Ethics for Spiritual Directors.* Revised Edition. Pecos, NM: Dove Publications, 1992. Included as appendix 1 in this book.

Spiritual Directors International. *Guidelines for Ethical Conduct.* San

Francisco: Spiritual Directors International, 2000. Included as appendix 2 in this book.

Print, Audio, and Internet Discussions

Abbott-Tucker, Lucy, Rose Mary Dougherty, and Janet Ruffing. "A Code of Ethics for Spiritual Directors: Prayer, Reflection and Dialogue (Parts 1 & 2)." Audiotape of presentation at meeting of Spiritual Directors International, Burlingame, CA, April 1995. Berkeley, CA: Conference Recording Service Inc. SDI95-004. Cassette.

Presentation of the initial draft of the document which would eventually become SDI's *Guidelines for Ethical Conduct*. Includes discussion of the processes used by the Code of Ethics Task Force and feedback on the draft from an audience of spiritual directors.

Abbott-Tucker, Lucy, and Timothy O'Connell. "Working with Ethics in Spiritual Direction." Audiotapes of presentation at meeting of Spiritual Directors International, Glorietta, NM, April 1999. Berkeley, CA: Conference Recording Service Inc. SDI99-007. Two cassettes.

Facilitated by a lay spiritual director (Abbott-Tucker) and an ethicist (O'Connell), this is an extremely helpful discussion of the application of ethics to spiritual direction. Some of the topics covered include dual relationships, boundaries, confidentiality, record keeping, referral, counseling vs. spiritual direction, directiveness, power imbalance, litigation, and legal requirements for disclosure.

Arnold, Kenneth. "Spiritual Direction Navigates by the Spirit." *The Episcopal New Yorker* 164:2 (April/May 1999), 1, 4.

Concise introduction to contemporary spiritual direction, including what it is, how to find a director, its relationship to Anglican tradition, and outlook for the future. Includes telephone numbers of several religious orders in the New York City area that offer spiritual direction.

Ball, Peter. *Anglican Spiritual Direction*. Cambridge, MA: Cowley Publications, 1998.

Discussion of the history and practice of spiritual direction in the Anglican tradition. Includes explanations of the relationships among spiritual direction, counseling, and healing, as well as a balanced survey of issues connected with training and professionalization.

Barry, William A., and William J. Connolly. *The Practice of Spiritual Direction*. San Francisco: HarperSanFrancisco, 1986.

The chapter "Disturbances in the Relationship Between Director and Directee" in this basic spiritual direction text explains how to recognize and deal appropriately with transference and countertransference reactions.

Beattie, Melody. *Codependent No More: How to Stop Controlling Others and Start Caring for Yourself.* New York: Harper/Hazelden, 1987.
Practical guidance for friends and family members of those involved in substance abuse and other compulsive disorders.

Benyei, Candace R. *Understanding Clergy Misconduct in Religious Systems: Scapegoating, Family Secrets, and the Abuse of Power.* New York: Haworth Press, 1998.
Considers the dynamics of clergy misconduct in terms of family systems theory.

Billy, Dennis. "From Silence to Silence: The Spiritual Direction Session." *Presence* 8:2 (June 2002), 38–43.
Excellent description of what might typically go on during an individual spiritual direction meeting. Especially helpful for spiritual directors in training and potential directees.

Boers, Arthur Paul. *Never Call Them Jerks: Healthy Responses to Difficult Behavior.* Bethesda, MD: Alban Institute, 1999.
An excellent, insightful discussion of interpersonal problems and conflicts that arise in congregations.

Brown, Sherlon, and Carmen Williams. "To Discriminate or Not to Discriminate: Culture and Ethics." *Counseling Today* (April 2000), 16, 40.
This article includes three case examples to illustrate how treating clients from different cultural backgrounds differently or in the same way can be appropriate or inappropriate.

Bullis, Ronald K. *Sacred Calling, Secular Accountability: Law and Ethics in Complementary and Spiritual Counseling.* Philadelphia: Brunner-Routledge, 2001.
Written by a minister who is also a lawyer, this book employs case studies of lawsuits to illustrate basic principles of law as applied to spiritual and counseling interventions.

Cattan, Mary V. T. "Giving Birth to a Ministry: Reflections of a Contemporary Spiritual Director." M.A. thesis, General Theological Seminary of the Episcopal Church, 1989.
In describing how she established her spiritual direction ministry as a layperson in a large suburban parish, the author includes discussion of dual relationships, payment, professionalism, and sup-

port for ministry. She presents a useful consideration of the complex issues involved in offering spiritual direction in one's own parish.

Childs, B. H. "Gratitude." In *Dictionary of Pastoral Care and Counseling*, ed. Rodney J. Hunter, 470–471. Nashville: Abingdon Press, 1990.

This article is relevant to the present topic in that it discusses the complex, both positive and negative, responses of people to what they are given (which presumably includes both God's grace and no-fee spiritual direction).

Church Insurance Agency Corporation. *Preventing Sexual Misconduct: A Guide to Resources.* http://www.cpg.org/insurance/publications/ index.html. Accessed April 5, 2002.

List of resources inside and outside the Episcopal Church to address abuse prevention and legal concerns.

Church Insurance Agency Corporation. "Protecting Our Volunteers." *Insights* (Fall 1999), 1–2. Available at http://www.cpg.org/ insurance/publications/index.html. Accessed April 5, 2002.

Liability issues as they apply to those who do unpaid work in churches. Includes recommendations for covering volunteers within church insurance policies.

Cloud, Henry, and John Townsend. *Boundaries: When to Say Yes, When to Say No to Take Control of Your Life.* Grand Rapids: Zondervan Publishing House, 1992.

"Many people have been taught by their church or their family that boundaries are unbiblical, mean, or selfish," states this book addressed to the general public. Adds Scriptural support to psychologically sound advice and provides excellent, clear examples of how and when to apply that advice. An outstanding book that I have recommended to directees. A companion workbook is also available.

Cohen, Marlene. *The Divided Self: Closing the Gap Between Belief and Behaviour.* Handbooks of Pastoral Care. London: Marshall Pickering, 1996.

Organized as a series of workshops, this book highlights the essential role of self-understanding in pastoral counseling and therapy. The author, an evangelical Anglican from Australia, courageously examines some of her own issues as examples. A group study guide and reading list are included.

Conroy, Maureen. *Looking into the Well: Supervision of Spiritual Directors.* Chicago: Loyola University Press, 1995.

Makes clear the essential role of supervision in helping spiritual directors deal effectively with problems in interpersonal dynamics. Includes verbatim case studies, guided learning exercises, and evaluation instruments.

Cooper-White, Pamela. "Soul Stealing: Power Relations in Pastoral Sexual Abuse." *Christian Century Magazine*, February 20, 1991. Available at http://www.anandainfo.com/soul_stealing.html. Accessed January 8, 2001.

Focusing on pastoral sexual abuse as the abuse of power between male clergy and female parishioners, the author takes an absolute stance, contending that "because of this power [differential], ministers must not ever get [sexually] involved with parishioners." She points out that "the pastoral relationship can and should be a sacred trust, a place where a parishioner can come with the deepest wounds and vulnerabilities" and calls for denominations to articulate clear standards and disciplinary procedures for boundary violations.

Corey, Gerald, Marianne Schneider Corey, and Patrick Callanan. *Issues and Ethics in the Helping Professions.* 4th ed. Pacific Grove, CA: Brooks/Cole Publishing Company, 1993.

This outstanding textbook for therapists and counselors has much to offer spiritual directors as well. It provides numerous case examples, discussion questions, practical recommendations, and suggested activities, and includes diverse perspectives from the current literature. The sections on dual relationships, transference, countertransference, and professional responsibilities and liabilities are particularly valuable.

Creed, Bill. "Dignity and Worth: The Question of Compensation for Spiritual Direction." *Presence* 1:3 (September 1995), 45–50.

Article written to stimulate discussion among members of Spiritual Directors International about whether, how, or to what extent directees should pay for spiritual direction. Is spiritual direction a ministry or a profession? What are the legal and ethical implications for each? Raises many questions, but (as intended) provides no answers.

Culbertson, Philip. *Caring for God's People: Counseling and Christian Wholeness.* Minneapolis: Augsburg Fortress Press, 2000.

Pastoral counseling text which includes a section on interpersonal issues ("Staying Safe in Ministry") that is insightful and relevant for spiritual directors as well as counselors.

Daniels, Jeffrey A. "Managed Care, Ethics, and Counseling." *Journal of Counseling and Development* 79:1 (Winter 2001), 119–122.

Addressed to counselors involved with managed care organizations, this article is useful for spiritual directors and pastoral caregivers by virtue of its elaboration on the American Counseling Association Code of Ethics, including up-to-date explanations of terms such as "informed consent," "confidentiality," "competence," "integrity," "concern for human welfare," "conflict of interest," and "conditions of employment."

Dewald, Paul A., and Rita W. Clark, eds. *Ethics Case Book of the American Psychoanalytic Association.* New York: American Psychoanalytic Association, 2001.

Elaborates on the association's current code of ethics with numerous case illustrations and discussions. Although addressed to psychoanalysts, a number of the issues raised are relevant to spiritual direction and other types of pastoral care as well.

Doubleday, William A. "A Response to Bishop Taylor." *The Anglican* (October 1998), 18–20.

Response to an article about sacramental confession. Raises and clarifies a number of important points about penitence, forgiveness, confidentiality, and pastoral relationships.

Edelwich, Jerry, and Archie Brodsky. *Sexual Dilemmas for the Helping Professional.* Rev. ed. New York: Brunner/Mazel, 1991.

Comprehensive and practical treatment of the issues of attraction and exploitation from a social work perspective. I especially appreciated the unusually diverse range of helping occupations and clientele included.

Edwards, Tilden. *Sabbath Time.* Nashville: Upper Room Books, 1992.

Comprehensive discussion of sabbath in Christian history and practice. The idea of a rhythm of sabbath and ministry is especially relevant to spiritual direction. Includes suggestions for living a sabbath day.

Edwards, Tilden. *Spiritual Director, Spiritual Companion: Guide to Tending the Soul.* New York: Paulist Press, 2001.

Basic guide to contemporary spiritual direction. Includes some discussion of issues related to payment and personal boundaries, as well as a suggested format for peer supervision groups.

Epstein, Richard S. *Keeping Boundaries: Maintaining Safety and Integrity in the Psychotherapeutic Process.* Washington, DC: American Psychiatric Press, 1994.

Excellent discussion of research and practice in relation to therapeutic boundaries from a psychiatric point of view.

Estella, Jeanne, and Andre Heuer. "Spiritual Direction in Cyberspace." *Presence* 3:4 (May 1997), 33–46.

Explores the implications of doing "Internet companioning" by recounting the experiences of the authors (Heuer as director, Estella as directee). Includes discussion of transference in cyberspace.

Ethics Task Force, Diocese of Newark. *Christian Decision Making: Commodity or Community? A Resource for Ethical and Moral Decision Making for Congregations.* http://www.dioceseofnewark.org/ethics.html. Accessed March 24, 2001.

Provides a brief, simple introduction to some principles of Anglican ethics, including the "three-legged stool" and deontological, teleological, relational, character, and pragmatic approaches to ethical discernment. Contemporary examples are included.

Fagin, Gerald M. "The Spirituality of the Spiritual Director." *Presence* 8:3 (October 2002), 7–18.

Points out the importance of the director's own spirituality in the direction process and discusses seven attitudes or approaches to spirituality.

Fortune, Marie M. *Is Nothing Sacred? When Sex Invades the Pastoral Relationship.* San Francisco: Harper and Row, 1989.

Appalling account of a real-life case of habitual sexual abuse by a minister and the astonishing institutional underresponses to complaints about it.

Foster, Jonathan. "Liability Issues in a Ministry of Spiritual Direction." *Presence* 2:3 (September 1996), 50–53.

Proceeds from the assumption that spiritual direction is "a ministry straining to become a profession." Details the policies and procedures followed in the author's independent practice with respect to legal issues.

Gabbard, Glen O., and Eva P. Lester. *Boundaries and Boundary Violations in Psychoanalysis.* New York: Basic Books, 1996.

To understand boundaries and transference in depth, go first to the psychoanalytic literature! This is the best book I have read on the issue of boundaries in therapeutic and psychoanalytic settings. Although not always applicable to spiritual direction, the insights into the dynamics of transference and the value of boundaries are most helpful.

Gallagher, Winifred. *The Power of Place: How Our Surroundings Shape Our Thoughts, Emotions, and Actions.* New York: Poseidon Press, 1993.
Examines issues raised by "the science of place" with respect to environmental influences on our behavior.

Grenz, Linda L. *A Covenant of Trust: For All Who Exercise Leadership in the Church.* Cincinnati: Forward Movement Publications, 1994.
Clear, concise explanation of how to maintain appropriate boundaries in working with children and adults in congregations. Includes guidelines for leading groups and a definition of sexual misconduct.

Grof, Stanislav, and Christina Grof, eds. *Spiritual Emergency: When Personal Transformation Becomes a Crisis.* New York: Jeremy P. Tarcher, 1989.
Wide-ranging, occasionally bewildering (to this down-to-earth reader, anyhow), collection of essays about many kinds of spiritual crises.

Guenther, Margaret. *Holy Listening: The Art of Spiritual Direction.* Cambridge, MA: Cowley Publications, 1992.
Graceful, beautifully written book about what the author calls "the midwifery of the soul." Includes a section on spiritual direction and women.

Guenther, Margaret. *Toward Holy Ground: Spiritual Directions for the Second Half of Life.* Cambridge, MA: Cowley Publications, 1995.
Spirituality and faith in relation to maturity, aging, and end-of-life issues.

H., Julia. *Letting Go with Love: Finding Peace of Mind and Heart for Those Who Live With a Practicing or Recovering Alcoholic/Addict.* Los Angeles: Jeremy P. Tarcher, 1987.
Book about codependency by an Al-Anon participant.

Heller, David. *Power in Psychotherapeutic Practice.* New York: Human Sciences Press, Inc., 1985.
Discussion of the power dynamics inherent in psychotherapeutic practice. The chapters on structural, verbal, and nonverbal manifestations of power have some applicability to spiritual direction.

Hiss, Tony. *The Experience of Place.* New York: Vintage Books, 1991.
Essay by a writer for *The New Yorker* about improving the quality of human experiences by becoming aware of and changing our everyday environments in city and countryside.

Holmgren, Stephen. *Ethics After Easter*. The New Church's Teaching
Series, Vol. 9. Cambridge, MA: Cowley Publications, 2000.
Clearly presented introduction to Christian ethical principles. Includes a comprehensive list of tools for use in discernment, as well
as questions for group discussion and a supplementary reading list.

Hopkins, Harold A. "A Lot Learned but Much to Discover." Address
presented at Interfaith Sexual Trauma Institute Conference, Collegeville, MN, June, 2000.
http:/www.csbsju.edu/isti/ISTIArticles/Bishop%20Hopkins.html.
Accessed April 23, 2001.
Interesting account of a bishop's growing awareness of the issues
involved in clergy sexual abuse. Points out that seminaries are concerned with the formation of the intellects of potential clergy when
"what they frequently lack is adequate insight into their own emotional (especially sexual) formation and behavior."

Hopkins, Nancy Myer. *The Congregational Response to Clergy Be-
trayals of Trust*. Collegeville, MN: Liturgical Press, 1998.
This straightforward, accessible booklet, sponsored by the Interfaith Sexual Trauma Institute, was written to help congregations understand and work through their reactions to clergy misconduct.
The chapters about transference as applied to clergy and congregations are especially well done. I particularly appreciated the con-
cluding suggestion that "looking for ways to empower the laity can
be a significant corrective" to the disempowering experience of
clergy betrayal.

Hopkins, Nancy Myer, and Mark Laaser, eds. *Restoring the Soul of a
Church: Healing Congregations Wounded by Clergy Sexual Misconduct*. Collegeville, MN: Liturgical Press, 1995.
Remarkably comprehensive collection of essays on dealing with
the "ripple effect" ramifications of clergy misconduct for victims,
perpetrators, families, congregations, other clergy, communities,
and the wider church.

Jeff, Gordon. *Spiritual Direction for Every Christian*. London: SPCK,
1987.
Introduction to spiritual direction by a British author who is
committed to making direction accessible to all Christians.

Jones, Alan. *Exploring Spiritual Direction*. Cambridge, MA: Cowley
Publications, 1999.
Revised edition of the classic work by the founder of the General
Theological Seminary's Center for Christian Spirituality.

Jones, Alan. *What Happens in Spiritual Direction?* Cincinnati: Forward Movement Publications, n.d.

Pamphlet explaining the basics of Christian spiritual direction, with emphasis on the presence of God in the process. Includes valuable comments on finding a director and terminating the direction relationship.

Krueger, David W., ed. *The Last Taboo: Money as Symbol and Reality in Psychotherapy and Psychoanalysis.* New York: Brunner/Mazel, 1986.

Fascinating and unusual collection of essays and case studies on the dynamics of money in helping relationships. Some chapters seem relevant primarily to psychotherapeutic settings, but a significant number are applicable to spiritual direction, particularly in view of the trend toward professionalization.

Langs, Robert. *Psychotherapy: A Basic Text.* New York: Jason Aronson, 1982.

The applicability of this book to spiritual direction comes mainly from the concept of the "frame," a metaphor for the explicit and implicit ground rules for the conduct of therapy. Langs argues compellingly that "the secure frame offers the patient the safest and most open conditions for free and unencumbered communication."

Lebacqz, Karen, and Ronald G. Barton. *Sex in the Parish.* Louisville, KY: Westminster/ John Knox Press, 1991.

Discussion of the dynamics of sexuality in relation to pastors and parishioners. Includes a number of clear and useful suggestions for ethical analysis that I had not found in any other source.

Lebacqz, Karen, and Joseph D. Driskill. *Ethics and Spiritual Care: A Guide for Pastors, Chaplains, and Spiritual Directors.* Nashville: Abingdon Press, 2000.

Breaks new ground with its section on "spiritual abuse." Discussions of ethical principles as applied to pastoral care, spiritual care of congregations, and spiritual care in specialized workplace ministries are also valuable. Unfortunately, the authors address clergy as professionals with the apparent underlying assumption that laypeople are merely recipients or consumers of spiritual care rather than potential sharers of responsibility for it.

Leech, Kenneth. *Soul Friend: A Study of Spirituality.* London: Sheldon Press, 1977.

Classic work about spiritual guidance in the Christian tradition.

Linda Julian. "On Finding a Spiritual Director." *Quarterly Newsletter*

of the Order of St. Helena 20:1 (March 1999), 1f. Available at
http://www.osh.org/ministries/Ministries(LJarticle).html. Accessed
November 17, 1999.

Exceptionally sound advice for prospective directees on what to
look for in a good spiritual direction relationship.

Lommasson Pickens, Sandra. "Looking at Dual/Multiple Relationships:
Danger or Opportunity?" *Presence* 2:2 (May 1996), 51–58.

Acknowledges a need for guidelines with respect to dual relationships in spiritual direction but questions whether psychotherapy's "distance model" is the best solution for this type of
relationship. Makes a good case for some flexibility and proposes
clear alternative guidelines.

McCormick, Kathryn. "Seeking a Compass: Spiritual Directors Help
Point the Way to a Deeper Relationship with God." *Episcopal
Life* 12:10 (November 2001), 8. Available at
http://www.episcopalchurch.org/episcopal-life/PrayDir.html.
Accessed January 2, 2002.

Brief reflections about spiritual direction in the contemporary
Episcopal Church.

May, Gerald G. *Care of Mind, Care of Spirit: A Psychiatrist Explores
Spiritual Direction.* HarperSanFrancisco, 1992.

The chapter "Relationship: Interpersonal Dynamics in Spiritual
Direction" includes a helpful discussion on how to deal with transference, countertransference, and sexual feelings in the direction
setting. The chapters "Disorder: Psychiatric Syndromes" and "Colleagueship: Referral, Consultation, and Collaboration" are extremely valuable for making referrals. I highly recommend the
entire book for everyone who offers spiritual direction.

May, Gerald G. "Professionalizing Spiritual Direction." *Shalem News
On Line* 24:3 (Fall 2000). http://www.shalem.org/sn/24.3gm.html.
Accessed July 15, 2003.

The author opposes commercialization of spiritual direction and
argues that "this modern movement to professionalize the ministry
of spiritual direction should be resisted in whatever form it takes."

May, Gerald G. "Varieties of Spiritual Companionship." *Shalem News
On Line* 22:1 (Winter 1998).
http://www.shalem.org/sn/22.1gm.html. Accessed July 19, 2003.

This article defines an unusually broad range of approaches to
spiritual guidance, including several types of informal spiritual
companionship.

Muller, Wayne. *Sabbath: Restoring the Sacred Rhythm of Rest.* New York: Bantam Books, 1999.

Exploration of the concept of sabbath that is broadly ecumenical as well as appealingly practical. Offers compelling discussions of how important it is to take sacred time off from our everyday activities, and includes a variety of suggestions for activities to help restore balance to our lives.

Newton, Lisa H. *Doing Good and Avoiding Evil: Principles and Reasoning of Applied Ethics.* Millenial ed. Fairfield, CT: Program in Applied Ethics, Fairfield University, 2000.

Casebook illustrating general principles of applied ethics, including decision procedures for ethical dilemmas.

Nouwen, Henri J. *Spiritual Direction.* Cincinnati, OH: Forward Movement, 1981.

Pamphlet with thoughts by a well-known priest-psychologist on defining and practicing the ministry of spiritual direction.

Nurrie Stearns, Mary. "A Time of Sacred Rest: An Interview with Wayne Muller." *Personal Transformation.* http://www.personal-transformation.com/Muller.html. Accessed November 1, 2002.

This interview with the author of *Sabbath: Restoring the Sacred Rhythm of Rest* includes and expands upon many of the important points of his book.

Ochs, Carol, and Kerry M. Olitzky. *Jewish Spiritual Guidance: Finding Our Way to God.* San Francisco: Jossey-Bass, 1997.

The first chapter differentiates among psychotherapy, pastoral counseling, and spiritual guidance and clarifies the role of transference and countertransference in each. As in Christian approaches to spiritual direction, "the real guide is God."

Ormerod, Neil and Thea. *When Ministers Sin: Sexual Abuse in the Churches.* Alexandria, NSW, Australia: Millennium Books, 1995.

Outlines real-life cases of sexual abuse by clergy and confronts the all-too-common tendency of religious institutions to avoid confronting this problem. Offers clear definitions and relates the discussion to Christian principles.

Overberg, Kenneth R. "Christian Ethics and the Spiritual Director." *Presence* 3:2 (May 1997), 47–56.

Discussion of moral decision-making methods in relation to the intention and content of Christian ethics. This discernment process is applicable to both directors and directees.

Ragsdale, Katherine Hancock, ed. *Boundary Wars: Intimacy and Distance in Healing Relationships*. Cleveland: Pilgrim Press, 1996.
Absolutely the most comprehensive, wide-ranging, and balanced collection of essays currently available on this topic. Includes contributions from recognized experts on diverse sides of these questions, with titles like "The Joy of Boundaries" and "Boundaries: Protecting the Vulnerable or Perpetrating a Bad Idea?" Historical, theological, and legal perspectives are thoughtfully set out, and gender, race, sexual orientation, and health conditions are considered. Anyone interested in this topic should read this book.

Rakoczy, Susan, and Graham Lindegger. "Psychological Competence for Spiritual Directors: An Interview." *Presence* 3:2 (May 1997), 20–32.
Conversation between a spiritual director (Rakoczy) and a clinical psychologist (Lindegger). Includes some useful comments about psychopathology, transference and countertransference, referral, and supervision.

Richardson, Ronald W. *Creating a Healthier Church: Family Systems Theory, Leadership, and Congregational Life*. Creative Pastoral Care and Counseling Series. Minneapolis: Fortress Press, 1996.
Study of religious congregations as interpersonal systems. The chapters on reactivity, triangulation, and being "a less anxious presence" have particular relevance for spiritual directors.

Ritter, Kathleen Y., and Craig W. O'Neill. *Righteous Religion: Unmasking the Illusions of Fundamentalism and Authoritarian Catholicism*. New York: Haworth Pastoral Press, 1996.
Includes three chapters of discussion of religion-as-parent and clergy-as-parent dynamics.

Rodgerson, Thomas E. *Spirituality, Stress and You*. New York: Paulist Press, 1994.
Brief, practical, and Scripture-based discussion of stress as manifested in our relationships, our thinking, and our expectations of life.

Rosage, David E. *Beginning Spiritual Direction*. Ann Arbor: Servant Publications, 1994.
A book addressed to directees, dealing with questions such as what spiritual direction is, how to choose a spiritual director, what to expect from the direction process, and how to avoid common pitfalls in prayer and discernment.

Ruffing, Janet K. *Spiritual Direction: Beyond the Beginnings*. New York: Paulist Press, 2000.

Insightful guide to more "advanced" spiritual direction issues, including mysticism, gender identity, and theological themes. The chapter on transference and countertransference is especially helpful.

Rutter, Peter. *Sex in the Forbidden Zone*. Los Angeles: Jeremy P. Tarcher, 1989.

One of the first and still one of the best books written on sexual misconduct by therapists, doctors, clergy, teachers, and other authority figures. Its discussion of turning an occasion of boundary-violation temptation into a healing opportunity is as valid as ever. My only complaint is that discussion is limited to man-as-abuser-with-woman-as-victim scenarios.

Schaef, Anne Wilson. *Co-Dependence: Misunderstood-Mistreated*. Minneapolis: Winston Press, 1986.

Solution-oriented discussion of manifestations of "the addictive process" in friends and family members of chemically dependent persons.

Shalem Institute. *Spiritual Direction: An Online Version of the Shalem Pamphlet on Spiritual Direction*. http://www.shalem.org/sd.html. Accessed June 9, 2000.

Brief introduction to the process of spiritual direction for potential directees. Includes advice on choosing a director and distinguishing between a need for spiritual direction and for other forms of assistance (counseling, therapy, twelve-step groups, local church programs).

Shepard, David S. "Finding Your Way: Sometimes Life Sucks." *Counseling Today* (November 2001), 25, 30.

Enlightening article by a counselor educator about his experiences in working with people in "hopeless" situations.

Stairs, Jean. *Listening for the Soul: Pastoral Care and Spiritual Direction*. Minneapolis: Fortress Press, 2000.

Excellent book about listening, caregiving, and contemplative living from a Protestant perspective.

Stout, Elizabeth G. "Building Your Practice of Spiritual Direction." *Presence* 7:1 (January 2001), 29–39.

Begins with the assertion that "spiritual direction offered in exchange for money is a *business*" and proceeds to detail how such a business should be conducted. Discusses how to set up an office; what to include in ads, brochures, and business cards; how to attract potential directees with speaking engagements, gift certificates, and letters to the editor; and what to do about billing, income tax, and insurance.

Switzer, David K. *Pastoral Care Emergencies.* Creative Pastoral Care and Counseling Series. Minneapolis: Fortress Press, 2000.

Practical how-to guide for pastoral care in times of crisis, with attention given to how to deal with boundary problems that may arise in these out-of-the-ordinary situations.

Taylor, Thomas F. *Seven Deadly Lawsuits: How Ministers Can Avoid Litigation and Regulation.* Nashville: Abingdon Press, 1996.

How to avoid common legal difficulties related to ministry, including allegations of sexual misconduct, fraud, malpractice, child abuse, defamation, invasion of privacy, and undue influence. Preventive measures are suggested clearly in each chapter. Explains legal concepts in an accessible way.

Westerhoff, Caroline. *Good Fences: The Boundaries of Hospitality.* Cambridge, MA: Cowley Publications, 1999.

Not a book about spiritual direction or counseling but a discussion of boundaries in a broader, community sense. Good evaluation of the eternal tension between hospitality and separateness, with examples of the necessity for and misuses of boundaries.

Willis, Robert J. "Professionalism, Legal Responsibilities and Record Keeping." *Presence,* 1:1 (January 1995), 41–54.

Proceeds from a conviction that spiritual direction is a profession. Discusses legal and record-keeping responsibilities in detail from that vantage point.

Woodman, Mary Ann. "Dark Nights." *Presence* 8:2 (June 2002), 31–37.

Includes a useful discussion of differentiating between the "Dark Night of the Soul" and mood disorders such as depression.

Zur, Ofer. "Out-of-Office Experience: When Crossing Office Boundaries and Engaging in Dual Relationships Are Clinically Beneficial and Ethically Sound." *Independent Practitioner* 21:1 (Spring 2001), 96–100. Available at http://www.drzur.com/outofoffice.html. Accessed January 14, 2002.

A psychologist in private practice argues in favor of nonexploitative, nonsexual contact between therapist and client outside the office.